D1475362

Embracing Easter Like Peter

Scattered and Sprinkled!
From I Peter 1

**Part of the Fresh Look Thinking
Devotional Series
by Christie Miller
Fresh Look Thinking Ministries**

In Dedication.......

As this is my 50th anniversary of
walking with the Lord Jesus Christ,
I dedicate this book to all those
along my journey who have
deeply influenced my life.

To my Young Life leaders (especially Judy Peterson,
Barbara Priddy and Tom Bates) who brought me
to know the Lord and discipled me in high school.

To Campus Crusade for Christ whose leaders
discipled me throughout college and challenged me
to love the Word of God.

To healing ministries such as New Life,
The Institute in Basic Youth Conflicts,
Cloud and Townsend, and The Genesis Process.

AND

To the many pastors who have preached
God's word faithfully into my heart and mind.

THANK YOU!!

Section 1

Introducing Peter and Easter

Introduction From The Author

Let me begin this devotional with something tough to confess. As hard as it is to admit, I don't think that the fullest meaning of Easter had really ever gone from my head to my heart before making these discoveries in I Peter. It is also strange to think that it wasn't from the gospel accounts but from I Peter 1: 1-9 that my heart-awakening about Easter took place.

Through Peter's eyes, I began to see Easter. How Peter embraced Easter, as a man who walked closely with the Lord and then actually saw the empty tomb. I'm excited about all that God has revealed to me in this study, and how my heart has definitely been transformed towards all that Easter can mean to all of us as it did to Peter. No longer do I have to sit through a Good Friday or an Easter Sunday service sensing that something heart-felt is missing.

This is all too wonderful to keep to myself. Also, as a 20-plus year veteran Christian speaker, God showed me that when I speak to a group, I leave after speaking. However, when I write, I leave a legacy. This book has been written to share my journey from just knowing the facts about Easter to really embracing all that God intended Easter to be in the lives of His children.

Peter, perhaps more than any of the other disciples, needed a deeper journey into Easter. He was the one who told the Lord that he didn't have to die. (Matthew 16:22) He was the one who tried to defend Jesus with a sword in the Garden as his Lord was being arrested (John 18:10). Peter was also the one who denied the Lord three times (John 18:27).

Then, after the shame of denying Christ three times, Peter went back to fishing. He didn't understand what Easter could mean to him in regards to his failures, misunderstandings, shame, regret, and purpose in life.

At the foot of the cross of Christ, we find only John, Mary the mother of Jesus, and a few of his other female followers. The other disciples, including Peter, had fled. They didn't understand the unfolding of the power and significance of Easter as Christ hung on the cross. They thought it was an ending instead of a beginning.

Jesus personally reached out to heal Peter from his choices to doubt, flee, and deny. Slowly, Easter and its fullest meaning unfolded before Peter's eyes. He declares his understanding in I Peter 1:1-9, and now this passage is doing the same transformation in my heart and mind.

My prayer is that this devotional will also open wide your heart and eyes to all that God intended Easter to mean to you. Easter was Jesus's gift to mankind just like Jesus was God's gift to mankind.

Peter's Declaration of Easter: I Peter 1: 1-9

Peter presents his Easter discoveries not in a gospel but in his book to the exiles who are being persecuted for their faith. As a result, we can discover so much about Easter from this passage.

"Peter, an apostle of Jesus Christ to those who reside as aliens SCATTERED throughout Pontus, Galatia, Cappadocia, Asia, and Bithynia who are chosen according to the foreknow-ledge of God the Father by the sanctifying work of the Spirit to obey Jesus Christ and to be SPRINKLED with his blood.

May grace and peace be yours in the fullest measure.

Blessed be the God and Father of Our Lord Jesus Christ who according to His great mercy has caused us to be born again to a *living hope through the resurrection of Jesus Christ from the dead, to obtain an inheritance which is imperishable and undefiled and will not fade away reserved in heaven for you, who are protected by the power of God through faith for a salvation ready to be revealed in the last time."*

In this you greatly rejoice even though now for a little while, if necessary, you have been distressed by various trials, so that the proof of your faith being more precious than gold which is perishable even though tested by fire may be found to result in praise and glory and honor at the revelations of Jesus Christ and though you have not seen him you love him and though you do not see him you believe in Him.

You greatly rejoice with joy inexpressible and full of glory obtaining as the outcome of your faith the salvation of your souls."

When I write my Fresh Look Devotionals, of which this is one, something usually stops me about three quarters of the way through. I look at what I wrote and say to myself, "That's a lot of words. What am I trying to say here?" This happened while writing this devotional as well.

That's when I stopped and prayed asking, "God what is it you want to say? In a nutshell, what is the message here?" What I heard in my heart from Him is this:

GOD HAS A LESSON FOR US TO RECEIVE THROUGH EASTER, AND PETER GOT IT! INVESTIGATE WHAT THAT LESSON IS!

Yes, I Peter 1 tells God's elaborate love plan for us which unfolded at Easter. I pray that you enjoy and be enriched on this journey into *Embracing Easter Like Peter* as much as I did investigating it.

Day 1
The Symbol
of Easter

Throughout this devotional, you will see that each chapter begins with this graphic of the empty tomb with the stone rolled away. This is the symbol of Easter, just as the manger is the symbol of Christmas.

On the cross, Christ called out "It is finished." While *His* work of winning salvation for us was finished, the Father God's work continued. He took the incarnate Christ, who was humanly dead, and caused Him to defeat death, be resurrected, to visit those who believed in Him, and to bring Him back to heaven to sit at His right hand.

We can't take this lightly. This is a feat that no other religious leader has accomplished in the history of the world.

This is something that has influenced me over the years while sharing the Good News of the gospel with others. Why would you want to worship a "god" that didn't have power over life and death like our GOD? A god whose tomb stays closed with no power over life and death is not our God. The true and living God conquered death. This is the God I want to embrace.

God takes responsibility for all of creation. His eye is upon us in our lifetimes on this earth, and with the raising of Christ from the dead, He shows He has command of what happens to our lives in eternity. I want to serve a GOD who is GOD, the One and Only true GOD, who always was and always will be. He is creator and lover of humankind Who has the power and plan to raise each of us into an eternity with Him.

He has risen! He has risen indeed. That fact holds great promise and hope for each of us. Christ did the work, I just need to "believe on the Lord Jesus Christ and I will be saved." (Acts 16:31)

My Personal Applications for Embracing Easter:

When I was in high school and had not met the Lord yet, I dated a guy named Michael Tanner. I fell for him head over heels, and during this time he was invested in discovering the religion of Buddhism. His search intrigued me because at this time I was also searching to see if the Christian faith that my parent's presented to me was what I fully believed.

One day, he was not at school. Puzzled and concerned, I went to his house after school. (We didn't have cell phones back then!) No one answered the door, which I thought was peculiar, but then I remembered his "escape place." It was a small 8 X 10 room built off of the garage that he had set up as his temple. He had several statues of Buddha, and this was the place that he read the teaching of Buddha.

Instead of finding him in quiet meditation, I surprisingly found him violently sobbing. Across each wall of the room, he had spray painted, "God is dead!" He was crying, "I've given myself to this religion and have gotten nothing in return."

His deep sense of loss and abandonment by his new-found faith in the Buddhist ideas caused me to think once again about Christianity and its claims. For a moment, I just stood there and looked at one of his Buddha statues. He was a fat guy who was now dead. He didn't have power over life and death. He hadn't claimed to be the creator of life nor the victor over death. He had just presented ideas and theories. This was the faith that was now disillusioning Michael. A god, a religious belief, with no power over death. No open tomb for the leader after he died.

I listened a little more attentively to my Young Life leader that next week. I wanted to know what powers Jesus Christ had. My heart began to be curious and soon was won over as that next year as a senior in high school I received the Lord Jesus Christ.

I needed to worship a God who not only lived but had the power over eternity and death. My God was not dead! He had risen from the tomb. He was a very-much-alive God, and I felt I could put my faith in Him.

Day 2
Peter
Got It!

Sometimes I ask groups held in my home or groups to whom I have the privilege of speaking, "With which follower of the Lord God do you most identify? Moses? Abraham? Joshua? John?" Overwhelmingly, the answer is none of these. It is Peter.

You mean Peter, the disciple who failed so often? YES!! I am so thankful that God allowed us to see his life transformed right before our eyes in scripture. This offers us so much hope. His life is a living example to us of the goals the Lord has for our lives as well as a hope that anything is possible because of Easter. Even my life can be changed because of Easter.

Peter often spoke without thinking (my mother often said I had that problem), he acted impulsively (that could describe me, too!), and sometimes he tried to take control of a situation when he was really clueless (and that's me, often clueless but needing to be in control!).

Perhaps this is why his written accounts, such as I Peter 1, are so hopeful to me. In these verses, we see the power of the Easter resurrection at work in reality - in the life of Peter. His risen Lord gave him a new revived hope for his life that had experienced failure in so many ways. He slowly yet emphatically understood what the cross and resurrection meant to a sinner like him. – or a sinner like me. He really understood... really.

When we read the gospels, especially Mark because this gospel was directed by Peter to a young convert named John Mark, we can see the amazing journey of transformation that Peter took. It moves from when he first became a disciple until the day he wrote the book of Peter.

Peter got it. He saw the power of Easter unfolding in his life.

His eyes were opened and he believed in the Lord Jesus Christ enough to die a martyr's death by hanging on a cross like his Lord – with one difference according to some historical accounts. Peter asked to be hung upside down on the cross saying he was not worthy to hang like his Lord.

That's quite a journey from saying Christ didn't need to suffer, to choosing to suffer an even more excruciating death than His Lord. His faith moved from shallow and superficial to deep and engaging – and all because of his eye-opening new understanding of Easter.

When I look at Peter in the gospels, I don't see his weaknesses; I see his strengths –sometimes just misused.

I believe there is no such thing as a negative quality; it is only a positive quality being misused – a quality that can be resurrected to serve the risen Lord.

When Peter cut the ear off of the servant in the Garden of Gethsemane (Mark 14:47), you could say he was acting impulsively. Yet, when you see that when he was called to be a disciple, he was also impulsive. He "immediately left his nets and followed" (Mark 1:16). I'd say that is impulsiveness used in a positive way. I call it faith.

Peter was the only one who also got out of the boat to walk on water to Jesus....impulsively. That was also an act of faith. When Jesus was on the beach after he had resurrected, Peter saw him from his fishing boat. He didn't even wait for the boat to come to shore. He impulsively jumped out to swim to shore to be with His Lord. (John 21:7) I call that enthusiastic faith!

Peter's life is an example to all of us to not lose hope in ourselves even if we have failed miserably in our lives. We can HOPE in the power of Christ's resurrection because we see it transforming Peter's life. We can rejoice in the work of Easter which is ongoing in our lives.

While Satan wants us to be downhearted and to feel like failures, the power of Easter lifts us into hope and anticipation for what Christ can do in our lives.

My Personal Applications for Embracing Easter:

While Peter saw that through Easter there was great hope for a person who often "got it all wrong," I also gained hope for my own life. I too was impulsive, spoke without thinking, and expected a lot of myself. To be honest, I let myself down quite often.

Reading about the transformed life Peter experienced through a risen Christ, I gained hope. There need not be any hopelessness, no person beyond rescuing by Christ in this world, and I wasn't going to be the first. Easter guaranteed that!

My life verse has become Psalms 18:19. *"He rescued me because He delights in me."* I needed rescuing, that's for sure. When I look at Peter's life, I see there is no way I can doubt that God CAN transform ME – a child of fear, pride, rejection, loneliness, defeat, and failure. One who has felt ugly, fat, and sometimes stupid, while having an always had a getting-into-trouble life.

Peter kept moving on, never giving up no matter what he said or did that was wrong. His failures didn't make him into a failure;

They actually made him more dependent. (He did go fishing when Christ was put on the cross, but Christ came and got him to reassure him that he was not rejecting him. Actually, Christ predicted that the disciples would flee the scene. John 16:32)

I have fled the scene, so to speak, many times, only to also be drawn back into the arms of the Shepherd. There was no condemnation, only a new challenge. *Follow Me. I can use your broken life. This is just like Jesus said to Peter, "Feed my Sheep." (John 21:17)*

I was just listening to Kyle Winkler speak about Satan's ploys against us. He noted that Satan loves to tell believers that this time they went too far. That their ministry is all over. That there is no hope for them.

Those are lies from the chief liar. Easter gives us the hope that we are never hopeless to have positive change and growth in our lives. I am so glad I can cling to this truth.

**Day 3
Peter Knew
Who He Was!**

Part of understanding Easter is knowing who we are in Christ. Peter knew who he was! He starts I Peter with these words: "Peter, an apostle of Jesus Christ." His identity was wrapped up in his role as an apostle, a chosen person to spread the Good News of the power and reality of our Savior. It is from this solid identity that he writes to us about Easter and his full embrace of all it means.

He accepted his role as an apostle boldly. Right after Pentecost, he stood before thousands and declared Christ as Lord, the Messiah, our Savior. (Acts 2:14) Many times he risked his life and was put into prison because of living out who he knew he was called to be.

He, like Paul, could say, "I am not ashamed of the Gospel of Jesus Christ for it is the power of God unto salvation to everyone who believes." (Romans 1:16)

This is the Peter who denied that he even knew Christ to a small group of servants. Now he was willing to risk his life to live out his role as an apostle while being an example to believers, to all of us who follow after him. A follower of the Lord Jesus Christ is our true identity. What does that mean?

I want to submit that until we really understand who we are as a reborn child of God that we will not fully understand the depth of meaning behind the cross and the resurrection we now call Easter. At first Peter was confused, but then he "got it." He knew who he could be as he began to fully understand the power of the resurrection of Christ. His life embraced an ultimate trust in who He was and his purpose. In this trust, he not only understands and accepts his calling as an apostle, but he goes even further. In the introduction to II Peter, he proclaims that he is also a bond-servant to Christ.

He knew he was not JUST an apostle, a called one, but that he was chosen, and in that ultimate trust he also CHOSE. He chose to fulfill his role as an apostle and then he chose to become a servant bonded to Christ. Ownership is implied in the idea of being a bond-servant. He had been bought with a price. Christ paid the price and Easter, including the death and resurrection, was a costly price to pay. Willingly Christ entered into a servant position and because of Easter Peter followed this serving bond-servant role.

This term according to the Webster's dictionary is a binding relationship of servitude or "one who gives himself up to another's will."

Peter could only do this because he now understood Christ's Lordship and all that Easter means. To be a bond-servant means to chose to be a servant, a slave to someone. In Peter's case, he was called to this position, but he had the choice to accept this post.

Christ was even referred to as a bond-servant to God setting the example for all of us to imitate. (Phil. 2:7)

Paul, James, John, and even Jude, the brother of Christ, caught on to what this would mean in their lives. In ultimate trust, they took on the role of bond-servant to the Lord as well.

Paul defined this term to say that as a bond-servant his purpose was not to please man but only to please and to serve God.

It means a giving up of the calling of the world for a bigger and more challenging calling - the calling to be a bond-servant.

That takes complete trust in the purposes and love of the one being trusted. Trust to this degree is a difficult ideal in our world today. Even in our marriages and families, we might find the need to cautiously trust someone who we love and who has pledged their love to us. Trusting a boss, a child, a friend, a spouse, and even trusting yourself is a tall order.

In the New Hope For Marriage weekend retreat my friend Deb and I facilitate to encourage women in their perhaps frustrating or hurting marriages, I present six types of husbands the gals involved in the retreat might have.

They range anywhere from Samuel, who was a mighty man of God who could be trusted to live in the power of faith and his calling as a loyal priest/judge to the Lord, all the way down to the challenge of being married to someone like King Saul who was an angry, rage-filled, selfish, vengeful and jealous man.

I make the comment to these women, "I can put both feet solidly into a relationship with the Samuels in the world because I can trust their walk with the Lord. However, I might only put one toe of trust (even the pinky toe) into a relationship with a man like Saul in order to guard my heart as it says in Proverbs 4:23. *"Above all else guard your heart."*

Peter knew who he was and who he could trust. That's why he could abandon himself to his calling and to his choice to be a bond-servant. He jumped in with his entire life – in ultimate trust and abandonment because he knew Christ was faithful and could (and can) be completely trusted. This turn-around happened in his life because he fully embraced Easter.

My Personal Applications
for Embracing Easter:

When I was a little girl, it seemed that my name was not Christie, but **CHRISTIE!!!** My curious and creative nature always got me into trouble. I seemingly could do nothing right!!! I heard my name called out quite emphatically with a negative flair maybe 10 or more times a day! That gets to you after a while!

I grew to hate my name as well as to begin to believe that I had no real purpose or value. One of the first journeys the Lord took me on in my new found faith in Christ was a journey to know who I was in Him –just like Peter knew who he was in Christ!

The Young Life leaders kept repeating Ps. 139:13-16 to me. "You are fearfully and wonderfully made." My brother used to say, "You are fearful all right. We always feared what stupid thing you are going to do next." (Oh, brothers!) And wonderful? Me? I surely had a hard time believing that.

I probably really didn't believe it until I found out what my name means. **Christie Lynn** means "Set apart for the Lord to bring people from turbulence into peace." I now know who I am.

That is why I now take people through their turbulent marriages to find peace and understanding. That's why as a speaker I am committed to taking people THROUGH difficult times. I have embraced my calling, who I am in Christ, and my purpose.

Section 2

Scattered!

Day 5
Scattered
Lives!

Peter not only intimately knew who he had been called to be in Christ, he also knew his audience. In I Peter he notes that he is writing to *"those who reside as aliens who have been scattered."*

For years I rolled right over this verse thinking this particular letter was really meant for these people who were being persecuted and had to scatter by moving to places like Pontus, Galatia, Cappadocia, Asia and Bithynia. I had never really been persecuted.

However, I began to realize that this letter is personally written for me as well (and for you) because all of us have also been **SCATTERED** in our lives. He first addresses the readers of this letter not by their city names but by what they were enduring. His audience is a group of people who have suffered. They have been moved on from what was their home, from a place they knew and where they found stability and comfort. Now they are aliens who have been scattered.

As I read this in my study time, I realized that this word SCATTERED means so much more than having to move (which we did six times in seven years ....and it was no fun!!!). Life today in our broken world is full of scattered circumstances.

People face divorce, job loss, children's rebellion, friend's moving, pastor's dying, relationships broken, lost dreams, and unfulfilled expectations. Each of these unexpected and trying experiences causes a sense of being scattered in our lives.

As I am writing this thousands of people are feeling scattered by the torrential rains and damage to Houston and in Florida from two different hurricanes in the fall of 2017. These people are feeling scattered to say the least.

However, all of these and many more hardships we face have a SCATTERING effect on our lives, and we can begin to feel like aliens. We have been uprooted not only from homes but from life circumstances we have come to expect.

Peter wants to give compassion to these people, but he does it in the form of a powerful truth. He has a special message to those who have been torn from their life-style to have to figure out a way to start again. They are aliens in a new land. Life is all new. Nothing is the same.

This afternoon, I am attending the funeral of a dear friend's husband. Her life has been scattered by this loss. Scattering comes in all forms.

I think about my friend whose husband chose his three affairs instead of confessing and repenting to stay with this faithful wife and beautiful children. This sort of rejection happens every day. My friend is picking up the scattered pieces after a heart-breaking divorce.

Oh the pain that comes when I think about the pastor who served his congregation with wisdom, devotion, sacrifice, and a time commitment that probably went beyond what should have been his boundary. What did he receive? A no-confidence vote in the last board meeting. His family is now scattering to find a new home, and a new church where they don't feel like strangers.

It's not hard to forget my friend who felt it was his duty to expose corruption in the government agency where he worked, but for his good deed he quickly lost his job. With four kids to support and a wife who was dealing with some health issues, he felt scattered and even abandoned by God. After all, he had chosen to do the hard but right thing in his job.

How about the teenager who was hoping to go to college, but was faced with the cruel fact that her alcoholic father once again lost his job, and she now has no support for school. Instead, she has to go to work to help support the family.

Then there is my friend whose husband is dying of cancer. She told me that all in her world feels surrealistic. She feels scattered, and like life is never going to be the same. She feels like an alien in a world that just continues to function "as usual" all around her. She just wants to yell, STOP, please STOP!

It is very significant to look at what Peter has to say to these people he dearly loves whose lives have been scattered and torn asunder. What would you say?

He not only acknowledges with compassion that they have been scattered and now feel out of place like aliens, but he also reminds them that they have been CHOSEN. "I am writing to those.....who are chosen." (I Peter 1)

Chosen? Chosen to suffer? Chosen to lose everything? Chosen to have their lives turned upside down. NO, chosen to receive from the Lord all that we will see in the next chapters of this devotional – all that Easter won for us. Through these provisions, Peter assures us that we can handle the scattered state of our lives.

My Personal Applications
for Embracing Easter:

Scattered! Oh yes! I can identify with that idea. You see, when it all comes down to it, I wanted a life that was smooth, a straight line kind of life. No bumps or bruises along the way. No surprises. Unfortunately, I wanted a life like Larry Crabb talks about in his book Soul Care where we love a life with no problems. However, this means we are seeking comfortableness instead of seeking to love and know God more.

Oh, I wanted my faith to grow, but without effort on my part. When I heard the idea of being scattered or "chosen to suffer," as Peter mentions, I thought, I really don't want to pick up a heavy cross. Can I be excused from this duty?

As a result of this mindset, when life did not go as expected, I was very quick to raise my fist at the Lord and say, "I don't like this!" When I first accepted the Lord, I really had no sense that I needed great tragedy or frustration to help me grow. I loved an easy life that I thought Christ would bring instead of the challenge of walking with God through "scattered" circumstances. That's why my fist kept popping up in rebellion when things didn't go smoothly.

It took quite a few years for me to see that God can't speak to a clinched fist raised in defiance. He can, however, minister and teach an open hand.

Now I realize that my life as I walk with the Lord is going to be full of chosen events where I might feel scattered and out of control. Events where God can teach me and use me. Fortunately, I have grown. Now, when life gets thrown into a tailspin, I simply pause and ask, "I wonder what God is up to now." (At least that is my goal response!! I'm getting better each day.) I call it the flow of faith.

I just attended the memorial service for a precious fellow-teacher who died at 49 from cancer. She was a woman who had this flow of faith. Never once in this process did I see her question God's decision to have her suffer. In fact, in the later days, her love and faith grew even stronger. She was a beautiful example to all who knew her to see the role that willing suffering can in our lives.

Strange as it seems, God calls us to suffer, and He never apologizes for it. We never see Him apologizing to Jesus for the pain He had to suffer on the cross. Jesus's example helps us to understand that suffering results in good outcomes. It is how redemption takes place.

Day 6
Peter Saw
What Was
Necessary

Peter GOT EASTER, perhaps more than the other disciples, but he was the one who told the Lord He didn't need to suffer and die. (Mark 8:33)   After the resurrection, his eyes were opened to see the reasons for necessary suffering.

God-allowed pain leads to gain.
Don't avoid it!

That could be the huge lesson Peter learned in his heart and life that translated into his depth of understanding Easter. Peter had definitely grasped this when he wrote I Peter.   Suffering was purposeful in the life of His Savior, Jesus Christ, but also would be purposeful in his own life.

In I Peter 1:6, he notes that being "distressed in various trials" will happen IF IT IS NECESSARY. In other words, if God has a greater purpose than the pain we have to endure, we may be asked to suffer –to greatly suffer – even unto death, but we know a greater good lies ahead. That is the hope of the resurrection.

I'm a rather simple person. When planning events with others I often ask the question, "Is that really necessary?" Sometimes my friends or family can get over the top with plans.....Martha-ism as I call it.

God only allows and does "what is NECESSARY." It was necessary for Christ to suffer and die so that He would release our sins and be resurrected to offer us eternal life. There is Easter in a nutshell.

Jesus knew His suffering would lead to the
glory of God's plan for mankind, and
He kept His eyes on the greater good.

Jesus used these same words of IT IS NECESSARY to the two men who walked with Him on the Road to Emmaus (Luke 24). At the end of their walk, after they had told Jesus the dramatic events of the Messiah's death and resurrection, not knowing it was Him, He said to them, *"O foolish men and slow of heart to believe in all that the prophets have spoken. Was it not NECESSARY for the Christ to suffer these things and to enter into His glory?" (Luke 24:25,26)*

The message of Easter is that God will do what is necessary for us to ENTER INTO HIS GLORY. Each day our lives may face various problems, or as Peter called it "distressed by various trials," but only IF NECESSARY for a greater good.

James tells us that at times trials and temptations might CROWD into our lives. Other times, God might give us peace on all sides as He declared to many of the kings in the Old Testament "And he gave them peace on all sides."

Ours is not to ask WHY, but to realize that these seasons
of REST and seasons of TEST, as I call them, are purposeful
for a greater good in our lives and for the Glory of God.

We need to fully enter into them, have an awareness of what is happening and embrace it as our Easter time of gain in our lives. God's glory is for us to become like Christ and that includes denying ourselves and picking up our cross and following Him. (Matthew 10:38)

We can be assured that God-allowed and God-chosen pain IS NECESSARY for our lives as well. It's important to ask when we are suffering great pain, *"God what are you teaching me? What can I learn? Is there fruit as an outcome of this suffering?"*

My Personal Applications for Embracing Easter:

I remember one time I had to discipline one of my daughters.

She was usually pretty respectful of the rules in our family, but this one time she had gone beyond what was okay. As I pronounced her "grounding" punishment, she looked at me as if to say *"Mom you know I'm a good kid. Is this really necessary?"*

I began to doubt myself as well. Couldn't I just let this one slip? Was it really necessary to receive a grounding for something I felt she had probably learned from already – just by being caught? I prayed about it. God revealed to me that at times we need reminders, we need the world to move out of our control so that we remember in future situations to be dependent.

What is necessary to bring me to a point that I realize there are bents, sins, tendencies, in my character – deeply interwoven into my very being? Only God knows the answer to that. As a result, He has taken me on several painful journeys where I easily asked like my daughter, "Is this really necessary?"

I equate it to the Israelites who walked around a mountain for 40 years - again and again until God felt they were ready to enter into the Promised Land. I have been around so many mountains, so to speak, more times than I felt I needed. God must have wanted a lesson sewn so deeply into my heart that I never forgot it. That it became such a part of my character that going against the truth I had learned would never even be thought.

"Is that really necessary" is truly a statement that lacks a trust in our God of love. He gave His Son to suffer and die because it was necessary. So if I lose a job (which I have several times), or lose a friend (which I have lost many over the years with moving), or lose a home (which I loved and thought I would live in forever), or lose a relationship with someone dear (which I have suffered because of death), or lose a boyfriend (who I lost to a drunk driver), or lose an engagement (which I had to a dear man), or .....and the list could go on and on......it is necessary because the God of all love is watching over my life to only allow, to only cause, to only sanction pain if it is necessary.

It comes down to trust. What is God up to? He is up to love and growth and to prepare me for the future He has in store for me. Is it necessary? Well, it must be because God is in control! He knows my past, my present and what will be my future. TRUST!!

I do want to note that sometimes as belivers we suffer at the hands of others who perhaps are not walking with the Lord. People who lack character and maturity, perhaps are full of anger and control issues. People who wish others harm.

Shepherds know that sheep can choose on their own to walk away from the shepherd. They also know that predators can enter into the sheep's den and cause pain and harm. That is a different kind of suffering.

We need to differentiate between the two. We may be suffering from our own doing, and not from the Lord's "if necessary."   There is a test to see if this is God-sent suffering or our not choosing to have boundaries. That test is SEEING FRUIT from the suffering. All God-sent suffering will eventually have fruit as a result.

Day 7
Any Other
Way?

When Jesus was in the Garden praying right before He was arrested, He asked God, "Is there any other way?" Any other way to provide eternal life for His creation? Any other way to bridge the gap between the perfect God and sinful man?

Jesus was asking His Father if their plan had to proceed. Jesus knew He had come to earth to die for the sins of mankind, but wasn't there another way, a less painful way to accomplish the same result?

The answer was obviously NO since right after this time, Jesus was arrested, beaten, and then hung on a cross to die the most painful means of punishment the Romans had derived in those times - and perhaps in all of time.

Peter may have heard Jesus ask this question, "Is there another way?" After all, Jesus was just a short distance away from Peter, James, and John as He was crying and talking to God in great pain. He may have been loud enough because Peter was just a "stone's throw" away. (However, for much of that time Peter was asleep!) Even if he hadn't heard Jesus, this question is right there on the surface of all of our hearts at times as well.

Jesus' example showed us that what you may have to endure, though it may be the hardest thing you have ever done in your entire life, is the "only way." The best and fullest results will come from this "only way" - from the "God's way" plan.

I suppose that if I am called "to take people through turbulence into peace" that my life will be marked with turbulence from which I can learn from God. I would say that has been very true in my life!!

Jesus is the "only way" to God. He stated there is one way to God: through the blood shed by the savior on Calvary's cross. There is no other way to obtain forgiveness and salvation. There is no way to be assured of eternal life but through the belief and surrender to the Lord God of the cross.

Peter heard Jesus say, "I am the Way, the Truth and the Life. No one comes to the Father, but by Me." No one. The only way is through Christ. (John 14:6)

Was there another way to spread the gospel so rapidly but through the "scattering" of the believers? Was there another way to create the earth and God's people but by giving them free will which resulted in our living in a very broken world instead of the perfect world that God had originally hoped and designed for us?

We can ask this question about earth shattering events or more personal, close-to-home-and-heart circumstances, and the answer is always the same. TRUST.

This *was* the best way. TRUST. This *is* the best way. TRUST This is the *only* way. We are trusting that God is a God of love and nothing He allows or chooses for us is not out of love. There is no

Plan B for our lives. Only Plan A. Jesus faced Plan A and suffered and died for our salvation. Yes, and God loves Him.

My Personal Applications for Embracing Easter:

Contentment with the way things are and the ways things are going has not been one of my strong suits in life. I'm so creative that I am always thinking, "There has to be a better way." I am always coming up with what I think are "better ways" of doing things.

Now sometimes, this type of thinking has landed me on a great new discovery. However, when it comes to relinquishing control in areas of my life that we need to surrender to the Lord, I also need to quit the creativity and start with the power of surrender.

I felt this the day I stood in the hallway outside my husband's hospital room. He had just had a stent put into his heart because of a major heart attack and blockage. He was doing okay, for which we were very grateful, but then all of a sudden he started to demonstrate stroke-like behaviors. There I was in the hall-way hearing bits and pieces of the conversation as the door was opened and closed for hospital personnel to enter and leave. "I think we have lost him," was the last thing I heard.

There I stood in the hallway trying to come to grips with the idea that I was now a widow in my 50's. I had to release all of my "do something" ideas. I was ready to scream, but instead I had a peace that I can't explain. It allowed me to totally surrender all that was happening at that moment. The Holy Spirit invaded my heart. If I was to be a widow, the Lord would take care of me, I was confident in that. God is still all love.

I was glad to know that they hadn't "lost him." He recovered and is doing fine today, some 16 years later. However painful and shocking that experience was, I see now the result it had. I have surrendered myself to the Lord in this area. This was God's best way of working this trust and surrender deeply into my heart to someday prepare for the loss of my husband and other dear people in my life.

I've also learned that God is never late, but He is also rarely early. If it is going to happen, why does He keep us in suspense. We sold and closed my parents home two days before we were going to lose it to the bank. We had it on the market for nine months, yet the sale and subsequent closing of the home was two days before the bank would have taken the home from us. TWO DAYS. Why wait? Wasn't there another way to do this without all of our wondering and worry - an easier way? God has His purposes, and the purpose of "this way" we may see in future years or not until heaven.

I struggled with this ONLY WAY idea when we got married. We both had our "only ways" of doing things, and of course we each felt we were the one that was right. Over the years, we have learned to respect each other's ideas and live in a mutuality that is so healthy and helpful. It reminded me of when Eve had an idea to taste the forbidden fruit that got them kicked out of the garden of Eden. After this, when she had an idea, Adam must have been leery to trust her.

However, I have learned that ONLY WAY ideas that come from God can be trusted. He will walk us through them, no matter how painful, because ONLY WAY experiences always have glorious results. I call this the "GREATER LATER" idea.

Day 8
Peter Knew
What Being
Scattered
Meant! !

When Christ was arrested and Peter saw Him being taken away, Peter's life became scattered. He tried to follow His Lord which he claimed he would do no matter what. "Though others may leave you.............I will never..." (Matthew 26:33)

However, instead of keeping this promise, he failed miserably. He denied Christ three times. Not only had his beloved Lord been taken from Him, but his belief in himself as a dedicated follower of Christ was shattered. The disciples had fled in all sorts of directions, and Peter's very life was also falling apart and scattering right before his eyes. With each denial and failure, his life felt out of control. He could not live up to what he thought he could be as a disciple of Christ.

However, Christ would never leave Peter in the shame of his denials. This is not the way our Lord loves us. Like shattered glass, He comes to put every piece of us back together. Easter won for us what I call "earthly resurrections" from our failures.

"There is now no condemnation for those who are in Christ Jesus." (Romans 8:1) The "NOW" in that verse refers to our life as believers after the power of Easter was released. I love the word NOW. It casts wonderful hope of a new start out to our souls.

In one of the most tender and perhaps life-altering moments that Peter had with the Lord, He released Him from His failure. It took place after the resurrection when he met with Peter on the beach. (John 21:17)   Notice, Peter's failure happened by a fire (John 18:25+), and now Jesus is meeting with Peter by a fire.

In this precious meeting, the resurrected Jesus entered into a thoughtful and uplifting conversation with Peter. He spent no time talking about his failures. I love that about the Lord. He is a NOW Lord not a WHAT HAPPENED, Lord. (Although, He does want us to learn from the past, we can do that as we move on in the NOWS.) Every one of our NOWS involves God's love expressed at Easter.

He asked Peter if he loved him with an "agape" (unlimited) love. Peter responded by saying that he loved him with a friendship love. (We know this by the Greek word that is used for love in each one of the three questions Jesus asks.) A second time, Jesus asked Peter if he loved him with an "agape" (unlimited) love. Peter again responded saying that he had "phileo" (friendship) love for Him.

In the third question, Jesus changes His questions and asks

Peter if he loves Him with a "phileo" friendship love. This is so significant because by it I believe Jesus was saying that he accepted Peter where he was in his love, faith, and understanding of the significance of Easter.

Christ knew that Peter had no clue at that moment what a resurrected life could produce. (And many of us don't understand this fully either.)

Peter would soon learn this power, though, as he stood in front of thousands of people at Pentecost and preached with amazing fervor about his risen Lord. (Acts 2:14-36) That was the power of Easter released into His life. It was the power of forgiveness and the resurrection power of a transformed life. I can just picture Peter thinking to himself, "This is my NOW!"

Embracing Easter as Peter did can produce an unlimited agape love out of someone who only thinks they can love with a friendship love. And it did. Peter got it! He got what it means to love the Lord with all your heart, mind, and soul. Peter's life gives us hope! It gives us great faith – an Easter resurrection faith.

For that to happen, though, we need to know what the resurrection really means. Not in our heads. Not just the facts in order of their happening. Not even just being able to tell the story.

It takes the truths of Easter moving
from your head to your heart.

Then God can empower our faith, work miracles through our faith, and transform our life to bring glory to God, just as He did with Peter. While Peter experienced the sense of being alone and scattered, the Lord came to him and reached deep into his heart and his shame and brought him to see his purpose and power. He could do this because of Easter. He understood that there was a before Easter and an after Easter and what that meant for a believer in the Lord Jesus Christ. It meant no longer would there be condemnation.

Note that in Chapter 3 of Acts, Peter preaches a second sermon and then in Chapter 4, he and John are arrested. They quickly experienced all of the Easter scenario. A life lived for the glory to God and one that included suffering.

My Personal Applications
for Embracing Easter:

When I became a believer, I was so excited about my new found faith in Christ. As a senior in high school, I jumped in with no reservations. I lived to share. I blocked out the idea that a life walking with Christ would have both glory and suffering.

Immediately I started praying for others. I created note cards with the names of classmates with whom I wanted to share Christ. Then, I would get up early and bathe taking these note cards into the bath with me to pray for them. Inevitably, that day, or sometime that week, the person for whom I prayed was somehow right in front of me where I could have a conversation with them. It was this secret time that the Lord and I shared. I prayed for a name, and then the Lord arranged for a time to share with them.

This continued into college, however at a cost. While many received Christ's love, others mocked and ridiculed me making my life unbearable at times. I never knew if I walked into a classroom if I was going to be received as a friend or treated as a foe.

What made all of this bearable was the fact that Young Life was highly accepted at my high school and Campus Crusade for Christ was respected on the college campus. I was involved in both, and this provided me with friends and a place to be accepted and recharged.

I think back to my heart in high school and college and can say it was 90% full on "charge ahead in your faith!" I firmly believed that God would hear and answer prayers –that lives were going to change as they met and received Christ. While many of the people I was able to share God's love with accepted it, many rejected me and I felt scattered inside.

When I had the opportunity to go to Denmark for my junior year of college, I traveled with a group of 50 others from my college. I had earned a reputation of being a God-follower and people warned others, "Don't get into a conversation with her. She'll bring up God in no time!" I experienced a lot of isolation from my group, so I moved over to the Danish students I met.

I can remember the joy when several of them received Christ – and the loneliness I felt when I was isolated from my own group. So while in high school and college, I had the Young Life and Campus Crusade group, I had no one in Denmark except the Lord.

Peter had the other disciples, and his first time in prison was with John. However, there were other isolating experiences when he only had the Holy Spirit with him. It seemed there were two sides to me. At times, I felt empowered, purposeful, driven, focused and filled with the power of Easter and the Holy Spirit. On the other hand, I recognized that I was a 20-year old who often felt a deep loneliness.

It didn't take long for me to realize that I had to stay centered in the Lord. I could not be like Peter who sank when he was walking on water because he looked at the waves and took his eyes off Jesus. (Matthew 14) My focus had to be sure and constant.

One time when I was wavering in insecurity and loneliness, God arranged for me to give my testimony in front of 1,000 Danish students through the Youth For Christ movement in Copenhagen. What a spark of encouragement hat was for me!

Part of Easter is knowing that while we have to face suffering, we are never alone. Jesus faced the scourgings before the crucifixion alone but with the power of God. The angels and the Holy Spirit were with Him to minister to Him. When Jesus said, "My God, my God, why have you forsaken me," His desperation of taking this all alone was heard in His cries. Because of Easter, that is finished.

We may be rejected by all men, but our God is always there with us. We will never have to say, "God has forsaken me," because He never will. As I experienced, there were times when I was surrounded by the encouragement of other believers. At other times, I had to walk the road of suffering depending only upon the Holy Spirit. My trip to Denmark showed me that God is always there even when I am alone.

Day 9
Reaching
The World!

Peter was well-aware of the suffering the believers to whom he was writing were experiencing. I Peter tells us that this letter is being written to *"those who reside as aliens scattered throughout the continent."* He never apologies for this. He never gives sympathy.

They had been uprooted from their homes and landed all over the continent. He watched their movement carefully, and I'm sure he had two ways to look at their pain during this time.

He was both compassionate and hopeful. Because of their new faith in Christ, persecution drove them from their homes and lives as they knew it. Their beliefs caused them great suffering, and they had to start all over again in their new homes. (Many Jews during World War II were noted as saying, "My life is here. I can't just pick up and start all over again." They understood what this felt like.)

However, moving and being scattered all over the continent was a part of God's plan. While Peter held their pain deep in his heart, he also saw what amazing things were happening in regards to God's purposes. The Great Commission was being fulfilled.

***On one hand he felt great pain for them and
the other glory to God for the spread of the gospel.***

The other day I was canning some apple juice. One of the cans slipped and dropped smack dab on the corner of my glass-stove-top. It cracked the corner, but to my horror I stood there and watched the cracking travel all across the stove top. I could do nothing. A zillion pieces of tempered glass soon looked like a map of tiny rivers.

It helped me to imagine what Peter might have felt (to a very small degree) watching his fellow-believers he loved be persecuted and scattered across the continents. There was nothing he could do. God was in control of what was happening in each of their lives. It was all part of His plan even though it involved great suffering.

Peter specifically names the new locations for these believers as he watched the gospel spread through them. He loved them and kept track of the movement.

This letter would have taken some time to travel hundreds of miles away to all of the scattered believers. Hope traveled from Peter with his prayers and with the letters. His awareness of their suffering is tender and personal. His awareness of God's plan was also dear to his heart.

When you look at ancient maps, you can see the places Peter mentions. There were about 500-750 miles north of Jerusalem, located on or below the Black Sea and north of the Mediterranean Sea.

Pontus - is 750 miles directly north of Jerusalem on the coast at the Black Sea. **Bithynia** - Lies next to Pontus on the west and is also on the coast. These two cities were active with trade with many travelers passing through. Many of these became believers and further spread the gospel when they returned to their homes.

Galatia - This city lies inland south of Bithynia and Pontus and it was a heavily traveled area heading to the coast and to Asia. The letter from Paul to the Galatians was written to these believers.

Cappadocia - A city that lies next to and south-east of Galatia. It also is an area with many people traveling through.

These places were located in what is now modern day Turkey with **Asia** being the area east in what is now Iraq, Iran, and Afghanistan.

Peter's beloved fellow-believers to whom he is writing have all been scattered because of persecution, and at the time, it must have seemed like a heavy burden to carry. Looking at it now, we can see God's purposes – the carrying out of Jesus's words in the Great Commission in Matthew 28:19-20.

"Go therefore and make disciples of all the nations, baptizing them in the name of the Father, and the Son and the Holy Spirit

*teaching them to observe all that I commanded you; and lo, I am with
you always, even to the end of this age."*

Being scattered to various parts of the world may seen disastrous
to your plans for your life. Over one period of seven years, we moved
six times. Each of my many moves over my 68 years of life has
resulted in being able to share the gospel with more people in my
new environments. I have to admit that during the times of moving it
was frustrating, painful, uncertain, an intrusion into our plans, costly,
and for the most part not desired. However, now that I look back, I
see God's hand at work.

Why and how did that happen?
Because of persecution, but more importantly because
of God's purposes for the spread of the gospel.
It was all part of Easter being lived out.

Peter knew this was all part of the Easter message. Scatter.
Spread out. Get out there to various places in the world. Spread the
gospel. That was Jesus' challenge, even if pain was involved.

In the history of the world during great times of persecution, the
Christian faith has grown by leaps and bounds. This was just such
a time.

Luke recorded this growth in the early church in Acts when he
wrote, "and they added to their numbers every day," – "....that day
they added about 3,000 souls," -- "many of those who had heard what
they said believed, and the number of men alone rose to about
5,000," -- "Large numbers of believers joined them, both men and
women." -- "the numbers of disciples continued to increase," --"a
considerable number of the priesthood accepted the faith." – "A large
number of both Jews and Greeks believed;" -- "they preached to the
city and made many disciples;" --"Many Jews and a great number of
Greek women became believers." (Acts 2:47, 2:4, 4:4, 5:14, 6:1,
6:7, 14:2, 14:22, 17:12)

The people were scattered to various streets, villages, cities,
neighborhoods, territories and across the seas and then eventually
across the oceans. Painful persecution and uprooting from their
homes resulted in the spread of the gospel just as Jesus

commanded.

Peter knew each of these people were part of the glory of the ever continuing Easter story - a story of love and forgiveness that needed to be taken to the world.

My Personal Applications for Embracing Easter:

As I walked through some mysterious times in my Christian walk wanting to ask, "Why? What's happening?" I learned that the "ah-ha" why realizations never came during the trial but after. The purpose of the cross and the resurrection of Christ was slowly comprehended by the disciples.

Now my life is filled with "this is whys" from the Lord. (Some I will learn in heaven!) Why did we move so many times? Well, my life is filled with people I have met in the Lord and with people to whom I could share God's love. All over the west coast, there are people praying fo me, people who have been touched by God's love through me, lives that have been changed.

The other day I was listening to the testimony of a forty-year-old woman whose mother tried to abort her. Miraculously she lived even after the affects of a saline abortion which is meant to burn and blind a child to the point of death. She has affects of this in the form of Cerebral Palsy, but she is sharp and can SEE life and God's love for her quite clearly.

She made a statement that resonated in my heart. "When a person is killed by abortion, it is not only that person you are killing. It is a whole line of people who die that day." That child could have given birth to more children and then given birth to more children and soon hundreds of people are living in this world being loved by God because one life was born.

After college, I was privileged to work for Mariner's Church in Newport Beach, California. I was able to visit a high school campus and was introduced to some amazing teenage girls. A woman from our church, Judy Brixie, lived across the street from the school and she opened up her home to us to have a small group on Wednesdays after school. About 12 girls consistently came to this group. Each one met the Lord.

Now these gals live all over the United States and one in a foreign country. They have spouses and children and even grandchildren. Over the years, those 12 became hundreds with tender influence in this world. I stay in touch with some of them, and that is a privilege.

One is the principal of a Charter School touching hundreds of lives. Another is a counselor in Arizona. The gal who became a flight attendant literally touched people from all over the world. Those are just a few of their stories.

The power of one person is amazing. My students are currently doing a research project by that name. They had to pick three people whose lives touched their world in some way. I want them to see the power of their life - their one singular life. By the way, in my 37 years of teaching English, I have had the privilege of touching thousands of lives. Some of those lives write me notes of appreciation I treasure.

Yes, one life counts because the influence of that one life is scattered in many different directions. You have to believe that YOU can have an influence, and that influence will be felt in broader places than you ever imagined. That is God's plan now, and it is the continuing plan of Easter being carried out. "And they were scattered." Your life will have an Easter impact today if your life touches even just one other life.

Day 10
Three Parts
to Consider!

In this passage (I Peter 1:1-9) we can find three distinct discoveries, and when we look at them, a greater understanding of Easter will unfold in our hearts and minds. Two will be shared in this Day 9 devotion. The third will be in Day 10.

PART ONE - REALITY

Peter takes only a few words in this passage to get to the painful truths that there is suffering in this broken world. How often preachers dance around the issues of life with lots of words and no compassion for the reality that most of us are facing.

Theories instead of the reality situations we face in life all sound good, but Peter knew these people's reality. He knew they were totally displaced, had gone through great upheaval, were trying to make a new normal out of their pain and suffering. They were scattered.

He doesn't go to the idea of "we have a hope in the future." He immediately recognizes the pain they are in RIGHT NOW. No starry-eyed look at life; first, he acknowledges the pain and the reality of the NOW is addressed. There was a need for reality and great empathy in that reality. I wish more pastors would look out at their audiences on a Sunday morning and speak empathy before they speak "get this truth I want to share." Empathy is the center of the Easter message and Peter understood this need.

As Peter starts this book saying that he is an apostle of Jesus Christ, I expected him to break right into the gospel message. No! He addresses with compassion the struggles that believers were facing at the time. I call this "empathy before content." Often we can't hear a message and absorb its full meaning until our pain has been heard and understood.   Close to my heart in ministry is the phrase, "A person can't move on unless they have been heard." Peter heard.

When someone *hears* - really hears - the pain we are suffering, we are then more open to move on to handle and grow from the situation. I have seen this true in so many people's lives, including my own.   Peter acknowledged the pain of the weary believers uprooted and traveling and settling in again - all because they stood for the gospel of Christ. His letter told them he heard. They can now move on.

My Personal Applications
for Embracing Easter:

I love it when pastors start their messages with, "I know there are some of you going through some almost unbearable circumstances right now. Many of which you don't understand, and you might have no idea right now what you should do about it. My heart is right there with you." What a powerful start to the reality of life.

We may all look good sitting in the pews, but the realities of our lives are not often as pretty as we look. I attend church in a very "religious" community. There is a church on almost every corner. Everyone looks good on Sunday morning. However, others have dubbed this community "the lying place." And why? The realities are buried. The pretties are often in the forefront, and many people are not honest.

Our church, and a few others in the community, are working at turning this around. We start in reality. Our small groups are full of conversations about the realities we are facing.   Prayers, encouraging words, heart-felt concern is given. We aren't afraid to face the fact that the Christian life is full of "scatterings" just as those first Christians faced - those to whom Peter was talking.

PART 2 - HOPE

After Peter addressed the realities of the lives of believers at this time (and in our time), he *then* goes into the message of hope. God had chosen them (and us) and because of the death of Christ on the cross, they (and we) can receive the power of His blood sprinkled upon them. There is hope that these problems are not an end but a beginning.

They can also receive the grace, mercy, and peace in abundance that God wants to give them (and us). Because of the cross, they have a hope for eternity. In fact, an eternal inheritance is waiting for them in heaven and nothing can diminish this assurance. It is protected by the power of God.

I think about the song that goes, "Is that all there is?" NO, that is not all there is. There is a reward, an outcome, a better life even after all we have suffered. There is eternity with a loving God.

My Personal Applications for Embracing Easter:

One time I was listening to the Bible on tape, and they got to the part where Jesus finds out about John the Baptist being beheaded. In my mind, I instantly went to the shortest verse in scripture. "Jesus wept." (Mark 6) Surely this news would make Jesus cry. Before this, I hadn't considered where that verse was placed in Jesus' life, and I thought for sure this was the perfect place for Jesus to weep.

I was surprised to discover that those were not the next words.

Those words were said when Lazarus had died and right before Jesus raised him from the dead! (John 11) A place where Jesus offered HOPE to Mary and Martha about eternal life saying, "Did I not say to you that if you believe, you will see the glory of God? I am the resurrection and the life. He who believes in Me will live even if he dies, and everyone who lives and believes in Me will never die. Do you believe this?"

Jesus offered hope to Mary and Martha, just as Peter offered a magnificent hope to those who were scattered.

HOPE
>a sure place in heaven is waiting for them
>there are positive benefits/purposes from testing and painful experiences
>God extends an abundance of grace, mercy, and peace to believers.
>the Spirit is at work in you to help you obey.
>we have been born again to a living hope.

Day 11
The Third
Part

PART 3 - PERPLEXITIES

For every idea I understand in scripture, I also come up with many questions. This passage brings up a few of these questions, so I will call them "perplexities." These are ideas for which I must live in faith and trust that God's love supercedes my confusion and my inability to see everything clearly. After all, we are to live by faith.

In this passage, there are several "perplexities" that need to be mentioned. I define a perplexity as something that just seems wrong. Something that God, in my human opinion, could have or should have done something about, but He chose not to address.

***The first is the idea that God had "foreknowledge"
that believers would greatly struggle
and experience scattering of all forms.***

He knew these new and faithful believers would suffer - and suffer greatly for their faith. He knows all that will and has happened to us. Just like He knew the pain that Jesus would suffer on the cross. He knew that just the thought of the crucifixion would bring drops of blood, not sweat, to His son's head as he prayed in the Garden of Gethsemane. God knew how excruciating the taking on of the world's sins and feeling temporarily abandoned by His Father would be for His Son. Yet, He knew the outcome would be even greater than the pain. Remember the "Greater Later."

In this I Peter passage, Peter uses such expressions as "the outcome of your faith" indicating that my faith is a productive entity which can bring about good results. He also notes that "through my faith" the promises of God are revealed and actualized for us. God and Peter present these "perplexities" in this passage of scripture which we need to acknowledge to understand Easter.

Peter jumps right into this passage saying God had "foreknowledge" of all of these things, yet He allowed them for a greater purpose. Not just to see us in pain. Not just to show He is powerful and in control. NO! To have something happen in our hearts and in our faith that would serve a greater purpose.

He also planned that each of our faiths would be tested, and not just a small quiz, but testing by fire, the ultimate test. This system of growing us up through various trials and testing – that can get hot and painful like when gold is purified – is perplexing to me. Peter tells us that gold is perishable, but our faith is not. It has more value than gold, and has an outcome of praise, glory and honor, as well as eternal life.

Yet, why this method?
Why must pain be involved in growth?

It's a perplexity, especially when we are going through the thick of it. However, our faith will persevere and come out the better for it.

Remember, even Jesus asked God, "Is there any other way?" In the Garden before He was arrested and faced torture and the cross, He wanted to know like I want to know. "Isn't there another way? Why only this way?"

When it comes to suffering, I want to ask, "Is there any other way to come out stronger, more mature, with a faith worth more than gold – in another way other than suffering?"

God gave His Son the answer. He would have to endure the cross. There was no other way. He gives us the answer as well. We must walk through "valleys with shadows of death," as we do quite often in our lifetimes.

In most cases of suffering, God never shares the why, and in that the perplexity lies. He is asking us to embrace the promise that suffering equals growth and a way to prepare for heaven. Easter was our example for this.

Yes, there will be suffering, and that perplexes me as to why suffering has to happen. God knows and doesn't apologize for the suffering His children are facing. He knows, yet He chooses to allow the pain to come into our lives. Rectifying how a loving God could not "change things around" - things He knows are going to hurt us - is very difficult. As we understand the entire Easter scenario, we will see this perplexity released.

My Personal Applications
for Embracing Easter:

Sometimes I just have a hard time with various decisions God makes. I was just watching a TV series where a woman lost her husband suddenly in a car accident. She told her friend, "God got this one wrong...just plain wrong."

I have been known to raise my fist a time or two (Or 300 times!) feeling like she felt: "God, I need to tell You, You got this one wrong." My version is to say to God, "I don't like this!" I don't go so far as to tell God He's got it wrong....but I suppose that's what I feel in my heart.

However, over the years of seeing God's faithfulness, I have come to realize His vast love and wisdom involved in the choices He has made for my life. God is love and His choices are based in love. They can be based in nothing else, because God is love...period!

He knew my friend would have cancer, my boyfriend would be killed in a car accident, my cousin's house would burn down, my friend's husband would lose his business, and that my friend's 11 year old girl would die from a brain tumor. He knew. That means He could have prevented it. That is still sometimes very perplexing to me.

However, I've always been the questioning child. "Why this way? Can't we do it my way instead?" I'd like to just use prayer. Pray to be more patient and loving. Pray to be more wise. Pray for God to "fix" a rocky relationship. Pray to have more grace and mercy for others. However, God's plan goes further than just prayer. We start with prayer and move to pain and then more prayer!

I often say, God does not give "FRUIT BASKETS" like what awaits you when you check into a hotel if you are an important person. No, the fruits in our lives have to grow in reality – on a tree over time and while battling the elements of this world.

A butterfly has to fight its way out of its cocoon. A bird has to do the work of pecking out of the shell. We have to do the works of faith and that involves suffering. It just is! To our benefit and His glory. It doesn't, however, stop me from asking about these perplexities.

About the perplexity of Easter. God loves His son, yet He asked Him to suffer beyond what most of us could endure. He knew it was going to happen. How could this plan be birthed in love? It is the major perplexity of Easter.

Day 12
Strength for
The Suffering

When we are asked to suffer, we are also supplied with amazing strength. God doesn't abandon us to face it ourselves with our limited resources. I have often asked, "How did Jesus endure the cross and the scourging before the crucifixion?"

I noticed four strengths that helped Jesus withstand the NECESSARY suffering of "being turned over to evil and sinful men," as noted by the angels to Mary Magdeline at the empty tomb (Luke 24:6-7). This happened when the words and the goal to "crucify Him" began to prevail and God allowed it because it was *necessary* for our salvation.

STRENGTH #1 - His strength for this journey of suffering was first given when He went into intense prayer *before* the trial began. He knew the need for what I call BATTLEFIELD PRAYER. This is where you have inside you the urge to resist what you know is God's will, yet you are praying for the strength to do what is for God's glory. In this case, it was Christ facing the Cross.

Luke tells us that God sent an angel to strengthen Him when He was in the Garden praying. (Luke 23:43) Not that the presence and strength of this angel didn't continue, but we don't see this specifically stated in scripture after this point. PRE-prayer is key. It invites God's power into the process of preparing to go through the (inevitable) suffering.

Twice He told the disciples to "Pray that you may not enter into temptation." He wanted them to pray not to be tempted even before they realized what might tempt them...such as fleeing from the Lord at the crucifixion which they all did. I try to pray this prayer "THAT I MAY NOT *ENTER* INTO TEMPTATION" every morning. (Luke 22 :40 and 46).

STRENGTH #2 - The second strength that He used to handle this horrendous suffering was to gather His closest friends around Him. He believed in the power of community. He asked them to come with Him into the Garden of Gethsemane to pray. He also confided in them His greatest inner battle and turmoil when He said, "My soul is deeply grieved, to the point of death, so remain here and keep watch <u>with me."</u> (Matthew 26:38) He was grieved and distressed, Matthew tells us, and He made that known to His inner circle of disciples.

I think it is interesting to note that they slept not just because they were tired, but because they were also deeply sorrowful. They hated watching their Lord suffer while not being fully able to under-stand or to be able to do something about it. Remember, Peter twice tried to "do something about it." He told Jesus he wouldn't have to suffer death, and then he took his sword to try to defend Jesus. He cut off the ear of one of the servants. (Mark 8:33 and John 18:10) In both situations, Jesus rebuked Peter. He was left not knowing how to "fix" this situation, and that was exhausting to him.

Jesus found strength in including community in his suffering. He was honest and vulnerable in front of them. He also set an example for us to reach out to community when we are in great suffering.

STRENGTH #3 - Also, a way to have strength in the midst of His greatest trial was to tell the truth but not to waste words defending Himself. He allowed Himself to be misunderstood and to be given over to the lies and accusations of these rulers and the evil men who did this out of jealousy. He simply said, "Yes, I am" when questioned about being the Son of God. Previously He had told the disciples that He could "rebuild" in three days (Math. 26:61) what man tears down, but he didn't say these words in the midst of the trial to people who would not listen. He didn't cast His pearls before swine as Matthew says (7:6). He knew it would be a waste of energy at that time, so he remained quiet, not defending himself.

STRENGTH #4 - I also noticed that He kept His eyes on the greater good. Even when He was being tried, mocked, and beaten, he proclaimed, "From now on the Son of man will be seated at the right hand of the power of God." (Luke 23:69) He knew the purpose. He knew the Glory of God would prevail.

I call this the ***GREATER LATER***. When we are tempted, we can look at the GOOD that will come LATER since it will be GREATER than anything we think is good right now. The sacrifice will be worth it. Jesus kept His eyes and heart focused on the purpose of the pain: winning the victory was going to mean so much for His creation - a creation He loved and came to serve.

I've asked God that my life could be a "sign" which is also translated "attesting miracle" to God's glory. That my "once I was and now I am" testimony will bring so much glory to God AFTER I have endured the trials and suffering I must face for the amazing life transformations God wants to take place in me. I want to be a testimony of God's faithfulness, but, as Joyce Meyers says, "There are lots of 'moanies' in our testimonies."

Easter had a purpose. The pain, the "My God, why have you forsaken me" was necessary for God's perfect will to be accomplished at Easter. It brought about a GREATER LATER!

My Personal Applications
for Embracing Easter:

We have all been told that the Christian life is not going to be smooth sailing. Trials can be expected. In fact, scripture tells us that we won't feel loved if we as God's children aren't disciplined. (Hebrews 12: 7 and 8)

I believe this. I know it to be true. I teach others this truth, yet when I am in the midst of something going not as I had hoped, I forget that this is part of God's plan for me.

I am often caught off guard. There have been times when you could say that I was enjoying a time of "rest on every side" like God granted to many of the Old Testament leaders. (II Chronicles 15:15) Then, out of the blue, a relational conflict arises, some bad news comes, someone misunderstands me or judges me, a car repair is needed, sickness comes, a failure on my part in some way.....and the list of the expected jumps into my lap!

Suddenly, my pride of feeling mature and settled, and my learned abilities to handle life's surprises fail me. I have immediate reactions of resentment, anger, and attitudes of "really, I don't need this!" come to the surface. Isn't that the way life happens even to Christians?

These things sneak up on us and our real maturity is shown by our first responses. When I hear about someone else's trials, I have learned to ask, "I wonder what God is up to?" However, when the unexpected comes my way, I whine like a baby! (True confession here!)

Okay, I do have to say that I am getting better. My first responses only last a day or so and then I buckle down and prepare to STAND against these forces of disequilibrium. My prayer is that when life throws me some curve balls, which happens quite often, I would be able to right away respond and not react.

Instead of saying , "Lord, really?" I want to say, "Let's go through this together, Lord, and I'm excited to see what happens in my life as a result of this challenge." That sounds kind of unreal, doesn't it? *Yet, if we fully believe that God is the blessed controller of all things, that God uses suffering to accomplish the GREATER LATER in our lives and for His kingdom, then that is a worthy prayer.*

Easter is our magnificent example of this. Jesus knew He came to die, but really didn't know the complete script of what was going to happen. He flowed with each step, trusting His father. Did He know there was going to be a Judas, that the end would be on a cross, that there would be scourgings, that there would be a crown of thorns?. Perhaps he knew the end goal, the cross as Isaiah stated in Isaiah 53, but not the specific details leading up to the end. His focus was on the end goal.

That is our lesson as well. The end result, as shown by Easter is that our GREATER will come LATER after we travel THROUGH the sufferings God has allowed into our lives for a necessary purpose. I pray that realization is my first line of response to hard times.

**Day 13
From Soup to
Praise!**

In the fall, I love making soups. Oh, I don't make just any soup....I call my soups enthusiastic. I throw everything in the kitchen into the crock pot . Then after it has simmered for a while, I spoon a small bit into a bowl for the taste test. I either come away with a resounding YES! or a NO, meaning it needs more of something!

This year my soup making process was taking place during the time I was studying I Peter 1, and so that was my first thought when I was trying to understand the TESTING and BEING PROVED process that the Lord sees is necessary in us.

Just like part of the soup making process includes putting the crock pot on high for a shorter time and then on a low simmer for a few more hours, so the Lord's testing and proving process happens with us.

We, like the soup, will experience a hot fire. At times that fire can be fierce and fiery, but it is only for a short period of time. In fact, one Greek translation of fire in this passage notes it to be "lightening." We may feel like we are being STRUCK by lightening – the fire and trial might come on so strong and so fast and so unexpected.

Paul talks about this in Ephesians 6:16 when he talks about the fiery darts coming at us. They come quickly, are unexpected, and they strike hard. God has warned us about this, so I shouldn't be shocked, but so often it catches me off guard.

Peter says that all of this is to prove our faith. That idea of proving means to examine, to discern, to see if we meet approval, just like when I taste the soup. I might say, "needs to cook longer" or maybe that it "needs more spices." As my trials continue longer than I would like them to go on, I picture the Lord examining me like I do the soup. What do I need? What is still missing? I am not thinking that He must be getting pleasure out of seeing me suffer. No, I believe He wants me to focus on "What do I still NEED to be shown to be mature and to be ready for the tasks ahead of me?"

Peter and James used the term, "may be found" when talking about our character development. (James 1 and I Peter 1:7) When God does a work in our lives, he keeps watching and checking and testing to see if our suffering has produced the mature character in me He desires. (Just like checking the soup for flavor!)

Peter says that my faith which is tested by fire like gold "may be found" to result in praise and glory and honor to Jesus Christ.

These words "may be found" refer to seeing Christ in us – that Christ's image might be see in us as we love others.

The proof is that this trial
and test has grown me up.

Notice, references in James 1 and I Peter 1 use the idea of "growing me up," not perfecting me. Growing in maturity never means being perfect, it refers to the state we should be at certain places and certain times in our walk with the Lord –to be ready for what we are facing now and for what He knows lies ahead for us.

Let's take this even deeper. These trials that are at work in us to mature us point to an idea of piercing according the Greek references. That struck me. Christ suffered a great piercing on the cross as He died for our sins. When I think of the piercing that God might have for us in our maturing process, I think of a piercing through to the truth, to the root, to the inside of my heart and thinking. What needs to be cleansed out?

When I have received a puncture/piercing wound, "stuff" comes out (blood, push, infection). When my heart is pierced, the "stuff" that is holding me back from being all I can be comes forth. When I am pierced, I need to boldly face the truths the Lord is pointing out to me. Those truths might not be pleasant; it may be a piercing that is very painful.

He was pierced for our transgressions. I am being tried, facing a piercing of my heart to test my faith and to go deeper to see what "stuff" in me is holding me back. What needs to be cleaned out. Trials have a master design from our Father the Master Designer. They are not pleasant as Hebrews explains, "No discipline at the time is pleasant," YET, they can produce a GREATER LATER; they result in something far more wonderful than gold.

What is the result? Peter spells it out loud and clear: praise, honor and glory to God. Our transforming lives can bring glory to God just like Jesus' life on earth and His death on the cross brought the highest degree of honor and glory to His Father. It truly is a GREATER LATER and not just for me or in me but for the Glory of God.

My Personal Applications for Embracing Easter:

I want to "grow up" to be more and more like Jesus, and for that to happen, I need to suffer. Plain and simple! That suffering might involve "piercing" from others, and that can be very painful.

David said in Ps. 73:21 that he was pierced within. Like David, people may try to hurt your body, but it is the inward attacks to our soul that often hurt even more. Jesus was pierced. Many in scripture were pierced with a sword and died. Others were pierced with internal attacks and needed to receive the healing God offers.

When these happen, we can become bitter or better. Each time I have been pierced it tests my love and power to forgive. It also tests my resolve in the Lord.

This morning my pastor said a powerful statement. "It is in the painful and bitter places that we work out what we believe about God."

When I have had to suffer "piercings," I have had to come to grips with what I believe. Is God a God of love? Is He all good. Does He have my best in mind for me at all times? Do I still believe that God is good?

These are questions with which we all have to grapple at some time. The "soup" of what makes up our lives includes our own sin plus the sin of others done against us, all coupled with the events and pain that the Lord allows to come into our lives. I can live my life as a reactor or I can live my life as a flow-er. (Not a flower, but as one who flows).

Walking with the Lord for these many years has taught me more and more to be a flow-er. Yes, God is always good. Yes, God always has my best interest in mind. He is capable of juggling zillions of people's lives at once for each person's best interests always done in love because God is love.

He is never too busy to see and to know what is happening. Foundationally believing this allows the mix-ups and the mix-ins of the "soup" of my life to be acceptable though painful. We can "taste and see that the Lord is good." (Psalms 34:8)

Day 14
Not Seen But
Believed!

Peter praises those who have not seen the Lord yet love and believe in the Lord. (1:8) Jesus said the same words when Thomas, the doubting disciple, declared his faith only after seeing Jesus' nail scared hands and the scar in His side.

Jesus challenged him directly by saying, "do not be unbelieving, but believing." He asks us to do this same thing everyday. However, each one of us seems to be in a different place with different needs when it comes to moving from unbelief to belief. The Lord knows what each of us needs.

Thomas saw the scars and then declared,
"My Lord and my God."

Mary Magdelene has a little different story. Her obsession when she saw the stone rolled away from the tomb was to find out who took the body of Jesus and for her to bind the body so that she could care for it properly out of respect. She was upset that she didn't know where they had taken Christ's body. When she finally looks into the tomb, weeping, God blesses her by opening her eyes to see two angels, one at the foot and one at the head where Christ body had been laying.

They asked her, "Why are you weeping?" She replied that someone took the body of Jesus and she didn't know where. At that moment, she turned and there was Jesus. He appeared to her. Not to John and Peter who had been at the tomb just previous to this, but first and specifically to Mary Magdelene.

At first, she thought it was the gardener as this tomb was in a garden near Golgotha. Jesus asked her, "Who are you seeking?" Hoping the gardener knew where his body had been taken, she asked him if he had taken the body away. She was ready to respectfully take the body to another place if she found it. (John 20:15)

At that moment, Jesus reveals himself by saying her name in His tender fashion that she had become accustomed to hearing. She knew immediately it was her Lord because "His sheep know His voice." (John 10) At that moment, she initially called Him "Teacher." However, after He spoke to her and told her His plan to "ascend to His father, My God and your God," she changed his name from "Teacher" to "Lord."

She was having a metamorphosis of faith. No longer was she looking for a body, she had seen the risen Lord. Jesus knew what it would take to bring her faith over to believing in a missing body to a resurrected Lord. He also knew what others needed.

John needed to come into the tomb with Peter and see the folded linen that had been over his face at burial but now sat neatly where the body used to lie. All four of these believers had seen the Lord, had walked with Him and talked with Him before His death and resurrection. However, each one needed a special something from the Lord to transform their fears into faith.

He knows what we need as well. John, Peter, Mary and Thomas were all seekers. That's when we have our needs for greater faith met – when we place ourselves in a seeking posture.

Now in I Peter, this apostle is saying to others, us included, that even if you don't ever see Him in person like these four, you will be blessed if you believe. Jesus asked Thomas, "Because you have seen me, you believe?" Then He declares to all of us who never had the privilege of being in the presence of the incarnate Christ, "Blessed are they who did not see, and yet believe." (John 20:27)

Peter heard every word Jesus said to Thomas. He extends this message to us when he says in I Peter 1:8:

"Though you have not seen him, you love Him, and though you do not see him you believe in Him."

I'd like to end this day's devotional with a story that author Larry Crabb told. When his father, a man of great faith, was dying, he told Larry that he had not felt the presence of the Lord in his room. Instead of feeling discouraged by this, he went on to say how wonderful that was to him. Larry didn't understand how not feeling the presence of the Lord on your death bed would be a good thing. His dad explained. "God," he said, "trusted me to believe He was there even though I could not feel His presence. That was a privilege."

He wasn't a "Doubting Thomas." He KNEW!! He knew God was right there whether he felt Him or heard Him or saw Him. God trusted Larry's dad to live in faith that His promise of "I will never leave you nor forsake you" was true.

My Personal Applications for Embracing Easter:

A friend's daughter is always doing gymnastic tricks when I visit. After doing a cartwheel or a forward roll she will jump up and say, "Did you see me do that?" I always reply with something like, "I surely did. It was amazing."

Then one time I had a need...several needs in fact. Each summer I do a two-week drama workshop with kids. I write most of the plays, and sometimes I can kick myself for writing into the script the need for a very difficult-to-find prop.

One such play required two BIG things. A juke box and a 1950's Harley Davidson motorcycle. (Why did I put into the script that it had to be a Harley? Why not just any other kind of motorcycle. Oh, yes, because a Harley has a distinctive sound.) The prayers began!! The kids in the play prayed as well.

Since I believe that the Lord partners with us in getting our needs met, I had to ask Him what my part would be in finding this motorcycle. That prayer took me to the Harley-Davidson Motorcycle shop in our town. To my amazement, they didn't treat me like a dim-witted woman. They thought it was great I was going to honor the Harley-Davidson brand in our play. They put me in touch with the original owner of the shop.

He was excited as well. He let me come over and record a Harley sound for our sound effects, and then he said that he and his buddy would drive up to Canada and get a 1956 Harley that he had restored and was not in a museum so that we could have it in our play.

He was true to his work and his wife and friends were in the front seats of the play enjoying every minute of the Harley being a part of the play. Each time I looked at that Harley, the Lord said, "Did you see me do that?" just like my friend's little girl.

We also had an amazing story about the juke box and once again the Lord whispered, "Did you see me do that?" These situations are like gentle kisses of love from the Lord. He cares about everything that we care about. He's never too busy. He seeks to bless us.

I don't have to SEE the Lord – I see what He does, and that is enough. I see what He has provided for me time and time again - things that seemed impossible – and workings in my heart and relationships. I have seen the Lord even though I have not seen the Lord in person because I see what He does in love for us.

Section 3

Not just Scattered, but...

Sprinkled!

Peter's Continued Declaration of Easter: I Peter 1: 6

Come be sprinkled by His blood!

Yes, we are often scattered in this broken world. Yes, we suffer a great variety of painful uprooting situations that cause us to feel scattered. . However, God's answer to our here-and-now brokenness is the "Sprinkling of the shed blood of His Son." That's just like God to provide a means for healing and strengthening in this here-and-now broken world with something we have to learn – something we have to discover.

He had addressed our woundedness straight on, but what in the world does that mean to be "SPRINKLED" by the shed blood of His Son? Most people don't even like the sight of blood!!

As Old Testament believers in God brought their sacrifices to the altar, the act of sprinkling the blood by the priest was a giving of an atonement for sin – an acceptance to the repentant sinner who has placed their offering on the altar seeking forgiveness. In fact, forgiveness in God's plan has always involved the shedding of blood.

However, when Jesus died on the cross, He was the final Lamb that needed to be sacrificed. He said, "It is finished."

What was finished? The need for man to find a way to pay for His own sins. Christ had just paid for every sin, past, present and future by dying on the cross. The altars were a temporary and incomplete means of finding forgiveness.

However, Christ is the permanent and complete replacement for all sacrifices.

The New Testament "sprinkling" in which Peter is referring involves the shed blood of the Lord Jesus. He was a sacrifice without spot or blemish, perfect in every way once and for all completing the forgiveness God offers for mankind. In His perfection as the Son of God, He is the only one who could fulfill this requirement for perfection.

What this SPRINKLING means on a day-to-day basis for us is told in this section of this devotional. It is the beautiful gift of Easter.

Day 15
The Power of
Being
Sprinkled.

Peter notes that the early Christians to whom he was writing were "scattered" and "sprinkled." The idea of scattered is a little easier to understand than the concept of having to be "sprinkled with blood." Jesus promised that we would have painful scatterings in our lives, but we could know that He was there to walk through it with us.

However, "sprinkled" is a term that brings all kinds of ideas into our heads. When I went to Sea World in San Diego, California, we got into the line for the dolphin and orca whale show waaaay early. We wanted to be sure to get a front row seat, you know the ones that warn you, "if you sit here you could get wet!"

Being sprinkled with water is one thing (and by the way we were more like drenched!!), but being sprinkled with blood, well, that image just doesn't set too well with me.

When Peter uses this term, "be sprinkled with His blood" it is being used in a figurative way, but it wasn't that way in the Old

Testament. Gloriously, though, when Christ died on the cross, He shed His blood so that we could all be "sprinkled" with the power of the blood. This included forgiveness and an invitation to enter an eternal life with the Trinity.

Jesus' words on the cross, "It is finished" were three powerful words with meaning that extended far beyond the pain of the cross. Yes, the painful act that Jesus allowed Himself to experience was over, but, "It is finished" meant much more than that.

It meant that no longer would we need to go before the altar with a priest so that he could sprinkle the blood of a sacrificial animal for us to receive forgiveness. No, Jesus was that once-for-all, once-for-everyone sacrifice, and His shed blood would offer once-and-for all the forgiveness He died to offer to us.

The author of the book of Hebrews spells the need for this to happen quite clearly. "Without the shedding of blood, there is no remission for sins." (Hebrews 9:22) Blood sacrifices were God's early picture of the sacrifice His Son would make on the cross. It all ties together.

The Jews understood this idea. They had to find and purchase animals without blemish or spot to sacrifice so that blood could be shed for them to receive forgiveness. To understand more of what it meant for the priest to "sprinkle" the sacrificial blood we need to look at this seemingly unusual Old Testament plan that God set up for His people to find forgiveness for their sins.

However, what is really interesting is to compare this process to our current need and means to ask forgiveness. Before we head there, though, (which we will in the next day's devotional) let's look more into Peter's words. In the context of the verse, Peter is saying so much more than "you are now sprinkled by His blood and thus forgiven."

In I Peter 1:2, Peter lays out a plan for living the Christian life. We were chosen, *"By the sanctifying work of the Spirit, to obey Jesus Christ, and be sprinkled with His blood: may grace and peace be yours in fullest measure."*

There is power in the blood. There is power in the Spirit. There is a process, an active on-going work, going on in our lives that utilizes these powers. In the Old Testament, they were to OBEY the laws, the Ten Commandments. This was a judgement of a person's spirituality.

Now, praise God, we aren't left to live a life of performance. We are left to open our arms and hearts to God's Spirit and the power of the blood in our lives. When we do, grace and peace will be ours — and not just in small measure, but in the fullest amount possible. These powers enable us to obey and to have the transforming work of becoming like Christ (sanctification).

The shedding of blood was only a part, the first step, of God's plan for mankind. He set into place a means for us to not have condemnation. Because of the shed blood forever sprinkled into believer's lives, and because of the promised Holy Spirit in our lives, we are more "more than conquerors." (Romans 8:37)

In the next chapters, though, we will see why we don't often feel like conquerors in our lives. We just might not understand the "way of sprinkling of the blood" and the power of Easter.

My Personal Applications for Embracing Easter:

As a child, I was raised to perform. (Yes, in the sense of drama on the stage, which I have been involved in since I was a child and am still doing today as a grandmother.) Moreover, though, my performance was to look good and to demonstrate to others that I was worthy, that I was acceptable.

As I look back, it probably all started when I was little. You could have called my brother and I "poster kids." We had to behave and "be good" to prove to my grandmother that my mother was a good mother. It was like my mom was on trial with my grandmother and we were the proofs of my mom's adequacy.

I was taught to perform for others approval, and unfortunately, this continued into my adult life.

While the priests of the Old Testament "performed" the sacrifices with the animals and the shedding of their blood, I had to "perform" to make an impression. I had to work to win my worth as a child, and those patterns were set into my life for years into my adulthood.

When Jesus said, "It is finished" He meant that no longer do we have to pay or prove or perform our way into His acceptance. He won it for us. We are loved, accepted, worthy through His Son, are liked and even enjoyed! Not realizing what this "sprinkling of the blood" meant for me, I have tediously spent my entire life proving myself in every venue of my life.

When, as an adult, I learned that I am free, it took a while to sink into my heart and habit. Because of the "sprinkling of blood" on the cross, I was free to be the person Christ made me to be. I don't have to spend my life PROVING anything – just loving Him and embracing all of the peace, acceptance, forgiveness, and covering He won for me on the cross.

There is nothing I can do to have Him love me more and there is nothing I can do to have Him love me any less. Nothing can separate me from His love. Nothing needs to be done to prove that He should love me. He does. He will. He has, and He did when He died on the cross.

As I write these words, I realize how long....L   O   N   G... it took me to realize exactly what that meant in my life and in my relationships to others and to Him. He wasn't looking down his nose at me with disapproval or disgust. He delights in me and enjoys sending His love to me. (Ps. 18:19)

The power to accomplish this for me and for you, took place by the sprinkling of the blood as a result of Christ suffering on the cross. Once and for all. There is no need to work my way into His good graces or to prove myself to others. His mercy and grace which was won for me on the cross.

Easter's "sprinkling" set me free from having to WIN the

acceptance of others. Yes, we might have people in our lives who expect a certain performance from us, but we have the freedom to discern and live above their expectations.

Easter completed all I need to be free from my old obligations to WIN His love and His forgiveness. My "Proving Days" are finished. While the priests in the Old Testament times had to go back again and again to the altar to "perform" -- I have been set free from performance by the "sprinkling of His blood."

Day 16
What Sprinkling
Means To Us

When a person accepts the "sprinkling by His blood," they are actually being born again spiritually. This process is all made clear in John 3 when a Jewish Pharisee named Nicodemus came to Jesus with a question. While he didn't know exactly how to frame his real question, Jesus knew what he was asking.

He stated, "Rabbi, we know that You have come from God as a teacher, for no one could do these signs that you do unless God is with Him."

Jesus responded not to what he was saying but to what his heart was asking. "Unless a person is born again, he cannot see the kingdom of God." (In other words, have eternal life.) This statement from Jesus took Nicodemus into a whirlwind of confusion. His logical mind, the trained mind of a Pharisee, could not absorb how a person could be born again.

Nicodemus responded by asking, "How can a man be born when he is old? He cannot enter a second time into his mother's womb to be born, can he?"

Jesus answered, "Truly, truly I say to you, unless one is born of water and the Spirit, he cannot come into the kingdom of God."

Jesus now had His full attention. He went on to explain that each person needs to be born once of water (through the birth canal with amniotic fluids) and then once again through the Spirit of God. We are born again through the Spirit of God through the act of Christ on the cross which involved the "sprinkling by the blood."

Because of Jesus' death on the cross where He shed His blood for mankind, we can now have a Spiritual birth that leads to eternal life with our Heavenly Father. Jesus told Nicodemus, who was probably still in a state of confusion, "Whoever believes in Him (that is Jesus who was the only one who could accomplish the Spiritual work for mankind on the cross) will have eternal life."

Then, do you know the very next verse? This whole story is in the context of the most famous verse in the Bible: John 3:16. "For God so loved the world that He sent His only begotten Son that whoever believes in Him will not perish but will have eternal life."

Sometimes we forget the context of that verse. It was said to a curious Jewish Pharisee but was meant for the world.

That is what the "sprinkling of blood" accomplishes for us. When we believe and receive the Lord's sacrifice for our sins, we are "sprinkled with His blood" which carries with it the promise of eternal life and the birth of our Spiritual life. Until that accepting, until that receiving, we are just physical and soul-filled human beings. When the Spirit of the Lord comes upon you with His "sprinkling of blood" a new Spiritual God-empowered world opens up.

With this new Spiritual birth, you are now a new creation with all sorts of resources to live in this broken world and with a sure hope for an eternity with a loving God. However, we still have our physical bodies and our very human soul with which to contend.

Christ comes into our spirit, and then begins to work with us for a soul and body transformation on this earth. Our soul includes our mind (all of those crazy thoughts we have that need "the mind of

Christ"), our emotions (which are both positive and negative, hurtful and healthy), and our will (which often chooses hurtful ways of responding to life.)

One of my life verses is Philippians 2:12 where Paul challenges us to "work out our healing with fear and trembling."

While the work of the cross for the forgiveness of sin and the Spiritual rebirth for those who believe has been accomplished by Christ, through the sprinkling of blood, the work of the soul transformation to be like Christ is ongoing. Paul must have known it would be a difficult challenge in this broken world full of choices that draw us away from God's ways because he noted that we need to do this with "FEAR and TREMBLING."

However, the work of the Spiritual rebirth in our lives through the "sprinkling of blood" is a gift. It is ours when we receive the Lord. Now this power can work with us to help this sanctification or transformation process to take place. New thoughts, new emotions, new choices can take place. However, this growth needs to be an intentional partnering with God and the Holy Spirit and the truths that Christ presented to us for it to be accomplished.

It all starts with an acceptance of the "sprinkling." Will you accept the sacrifice, the blood sacrifice, given to you by the Lord Jesus for all of mankind? This is what Easter is all about!

My Personal Applications for Embracing Easter:

When I was growing up, we attended a very socially-oriented church. I can't remember the gospel ever being shared. Each Sunday we would receive a set of new instructions for living the good life. What I call my "should do's."

That was hard (no impossible) because I was a curious, active, adventurous soul who never seemed to be able to please members of my family. I had two grandmothers who cared for me often. My sweet grandmother was not really religious.

However, my other grandmother was very religious and legalistic. My legalistic grandmother once spanked me when I was visiting her for playing the card game *Old Maid* and *Go Fish* on the front porch with a neighbor girl.

The sad thing about that was the reaction of the neighbor girl. While we were playing cards, she was sharing with me while we were playing cards that her parents were getting a divorce and she was feeling quite afraid and lonely. I was going to invite her to my church on Sunday. At least she might feel loved in our very social church. However, that never happened because I was grounded from playing with her ever again in addition to getting a spanking.

I suppose that incident marked my heart with confusion about what Christianity really meant. In my mind, it boiled down to a bunch of rules we needed to follow to be perfect enough for God to accept us. Playing cards was obviously out! Even a childish game like *Go Fish.*

My parents required that we go to church with them. I remember in the fifth grade I had a Sunday School teacher who was beautiful, gracious, and caring. She had won my heart. I was about ready to say YES in my heart to Christianity even though I had no idea what that meant at the time. I was going to tell her that next Sunday morning, but she wasn't there. Instead, I heard that she up and left her husband and three kids to run away with another man. So much for my faith in Christianity at that age.

When my brother and I were in middle school and high school, we had a large home, so Young Life approached us to host the Monday night Young Life meetings. They had found a greater response from teens if we met in a home than in a church or elsewhere. My parents, social as they were, opened the doors to 75 kids every Monday night.

It was through this ministry that I actually came to hear about what Jesus death on the cross actually meant. It was my senior year before I surrendered my heart and total self to this Jesus who knew me, loved me and sacrificed for me. I was "sprinkled".....and it made all the difference in the world to me.

I was now born again and full of a new life in the Spirit. I quit judging Christianity by other people's lives and began to look at the life that really counted – the sacrificial life of love of the Lord Jesus Christ. That journey was only the most important step I have taken in my life.

I now needed to let God invade my soul. That was a challenge because I was an emotional basket case. The joke told about me at this time was that my emotional mood would change from the time a young man opened his car door for me to take me on a date to the time he got around the car to let himself in. Roller Coast was a good word to define my emotions. God had His work cut out for Him.

That's why the Philippians 2:12 verse is so powerful to me. *"Work out* (yes, my continued transformation is like a work out that draws sweat and pain!) *your healing* (and I needed a lot of healing and I had to acknowledge my specific areas that needed healing) *with fear and trembling* (I realized that there were some things planted in my soul that were very dangerous and counter-productive to my walk with Christ. I needed to fear what they could do to destroy me....like the seeds planted on the wrong soil. (Matthew 13:4)

And so.....the journey has continued these 50 years. Healing the wounds of the past, keeping up with the wounds of the present, and grabbing a tighter and tighter hold onto the Lord for all the future brings. The transformation of my soul has been nothing less than a miracle....nothing less than the power of Easter and the "sprinkling' of blood on a life. It can also be yours.

Day 17
Confessing First!

In the Old Testament, the people were dependent upon the Priest performing a religious ritual to obtain their forgiveness. When you look at all of the steps that it took for this cleansing from sin to take place, you will see it was an exacting and grueling procedure.

First, because God is a holy God, the priests had to cleanse the altar of the Lord (which represented the presence of the Lord - a holy place) as well as consecrating and purifying themselves to be able to perform this religious ceremony. This was no easy task as it took seven days as well as a cleansing period for the priests.

Once this was complete, the people could bring their sacrifices for the shedding of blood. However, it is really significant to note that before the lamb (or other animals) were sacrificed, the people had to confess honestly before the Lord.

Exodus 24:6-8 tells the procedure. "Moses took half of the blood and put it into basins, and the other half of the blood he sprinkled on the altar. Then he took the book of the covenant and read it in the hearing of the people. They responded by saying, " 'All that the Lord has spoken we will do, and we will be obedient.'"

THEN... THEN... catch this. "THEN Moses took the blood and sprinkled it on the people or on the altar saying, 'Behold the blood of the covenant which the Lord has made with you in accordance with all of these words.'"

Before we think that being forgiven is a "piece of cake," we need to see the responsibility of ownership of our sins. Peter saw this. He said, "to obey Jesus Christ and be sprinkled with His blood." (1:6)---

Page 67

in that order. He presents the process of forgiveness in that same order as Moses. Confession and then forgiveness.

Own your sin, and then receive the forgiveness. It is not just feeling badly about your sin. It is owning it. Jesus said to the woman brought to Jesus after being caught in adultery, "where are those who condemn you. Neither do I condemn you. Go and sin no more. He didn't just say "Go, you are forgiven." His words implied, "Go and realize you need to own your behavior and your choices. What you did was sin. You are not getting off without realizing your part in this. Own it. It is yours."

The beauty of Easter is that we can own it and then believe and receive the forgiveness Christ died to give. We are sprinkled with the power of the cross where Christ shed His precious blood for us. That gives us the freedom and the roadway to own our stuff and not have to stay in shame and regret.

This is a hard concept to grasp. I am forgiven once and for all, yet I need to confess my sins. Many Christians I know say in pride, "Well, I don't need to confess. I am already forgiven –past present and future sins." While that is true that our past, present, and future sins are forgiven, we also need to own them.

We own them by admitting them to the Lord and out loud like at the altar in the Old Testament times. "All that the Lord has spoken we will do, and we will be obedient." (Exodus 24:8)

There is an additional part of confession that is often left untold in the Christian church. Most of us know that we need to confess to the Lord, but we also need to realize that James tells us that confessing to one another brings healing into our lives. Perhaps that was why coming before the altar and the priest in the tabernacle was so important.

However, now the temple curtain has been torn and we can come right before the thrown of grace to confess our sins. No need for the sacrifice of animals. Jesus paid it all. We do need to confess our sins to God, but James adds that we need to confess our sins to one another. "Confess your sins, one to another, and you will be healed." (James 5:13-16) Confessing to others, out loud in humility will bring healing.

Dr. Henry Cloud defines repenting as "really getting it." We really see how the actions and attitudes we have had in our lives are affecting us and our relationships. They are grieving God.

This means really having an ah-ha moment of embracing what we did that was unhealthy, rebellious, selfish, fearful, betraying, etc. – acts that are not dependent upon Christ.

Hebrews talks about the "sin that does so easily beset us." Notice the word is not SINS - but SIN. There is one besetting sin that affects all of us. That sin is the sin of having an independent spirit - of not clinging to and being dependent upon Christ. That needs to be realized and confessed.

Our sins are covered by the "sprinkling of blood" we receive from Christ, however for real healing to occur we need to confess first. With this "sprinkling of blood," the result of Easter, a new power, a new hope, and the freedom of forgiveness can place in our lives. It is one thing to be forgiven and another to live in the freedom and power of forgiveness because we are willing to specifically confess our sins.

This is what Easter won for us - the freedom to be honest.

My Personal Applications for Embracing Easter:

As I have gotten older, I have realized that asking forgiveness for specific and stated out loud sins has become powerful in my life. In fact, in my family, we don't "apologize" or say, "I'm sorry." We ask forgiveness for a specific offense. We own it. It grates me when I hear little children and adults just saying "I'm sorry."

I'm sorry just says you are sorry that you got caught –I'm sorry you feel badly (although that's your problem) – or I'm sorry that you are so offended that I made a mistake. I'm sorry you can't handle me the way I am.

No, "I'm sorry" are words we avoid. We say to one another, "Please forgive me for........." (And state the specific sin.) I have had to confess many things. Please forgive me for lying, for being selfish and spending money that we had set aside for something else, for yelling and being angry when I was inconvenienced, for judging you unfairly, for trying to control you, for not connecting with you in your time of need, for saying those critical words, for spreading gossip, for not coming to you first about a problem, for abandoning you.....and the list can go on and on.

How powerful is a confession that states the specific offense when confessing. There is power and responsibility in those words. Honest and specific confessions said to the Lord and/or to others releases the power given to us by the sprinkling of the blood of forgiveness into our lives. It gives us freedom and peace.

Yet, think about it. I'll bet that you can count on one hand the number of people who have come to you and formally asked your forgiveness for a specific sin. Other than my family, I can count on one hand the others who have asked for my forgiveness after offending me. Not that I am keeping score, but in reflecting back on this in my life, this is what I am realizing.

What a travesty. Our entire Christian faith is wrapped around the cross and the blood-shedding, life-sacrificing act of Christ on the cross to offer us forgiveness. However, we often refuse to forgive, feel that the sin against us was too great, or our pride is so strong we won't own our sin and ask for forgiveness. The very core of our Christian faith is brushed aside.

When, however, I have owned a sin and have confessed it, God uses that humility and honesty in magnificent ways. I would like to state emphatically that every time I have gone to someone to ask forgiveness, the relationship has turned around (except in one case where the person would not forgive me for something I said about their daughter) and become stronger and closer. Owning my specific sin has been a journey which now reaps amazing blessings.

When we sin against someone, a wall of offense is put up between us, and the greatest power to take down that wall is a personal, one-on-one request for forgiveness stating specifically the sin you have committed against them.

Here's an example:

State it - "I have sinned"

Specifically - "I complained to others before coming to you about a hurt I was feeling."

Ask forgiveness - "I would like to ask you to forgive me."

Take responsibility - "I have also gone to the others and I have asked their forgiveness and have cleared up the truths of this situation with them.

Commit to change - I learned a lot from this experience and believe that in the future I will know to go to the person involved first."

Then request - "Would you forgive me?"

And with that....let the healing begin. Let the walls come down, let the freedom that comes from forgiveness enter and heal your life. Let the humility you have expressed touch another person's life with the power of God.

Day 18
What If
Forgiveness
Is Refused?

"For God so loved the world, He gave His only begotten Son....." to die and offer to those who will believe His "sprinkled blood." To those who WILL believe.

However, there are those who won't believe. They just won't see the need for forgiveness or be willing to accept this gift from God. I am thinking of my friend's husband who even at his dying breath pushed the love of God away. I am thinking of a relative who everyday mocks those in his family who believe. I am thinking of friends who define God as they *want* to see him. Of course, there is no messy "sprinkling of blood" involved in their god.

To these people I say, YOU ARE TRAPPED! You are not free. You are caged in your own wounds and pride. I believe that when I pray for friends and family, the Holy Spirit works overtime on their hearts and minds. Their power to resist Him is so tragic. They are holding onto something that is leading them to destruction.

"There is a way that seems right to a man, but that way is death." Notice this verse in Proverbs is repeated twice for emphasis. (Proverbs 14:12 and 16:25). Yet many people continue to move away instead of towards the Savior. They won't accept the "sprinkling of blood" offered to them no matter how needy they become.

In the Old Testament, there is a story of a powerful officer of the king named Naaman who was stricken with leprosy. He was told by a Jewish servant girl that if he went to the prophet Elijah, he could be healed. After being granted leave to go from the King, he loaded up all sorts of presents for the prophet to trade or pay him for his healing. (II Kings 5:1)

When he arrived near the prophet's home, he was met by Elijah's servant, Gehazi.   He told Naaman that Elijah told him to instruct this officer to dip himself in the Jordan River seven times.

That was an outlandish idea to Naaman, much like being "sprinkled with blood" is to many people today. His pride reared its ugly head. He thought how foolish he was for traveling so far as there were much cleaner rivers closer to home if dipping himself in a river was to be his cure.

He was about to leave when His servants appealed to him. What would it hurt to try?   He relented and dipped himself seven times in the river. He was healed. So I ask, did the healing come from the Jordan or from the obedience?

How many powerful in-their-own right people would not have listened to their servant. Who would have left without even giving it a try? Psalms tells us to "Taste and see that the Lord is good." You have to taste to know.   (Psalms 34:8)

My friend told me about some missionaries in Muslim countries who go to the homes of various Muslims and ask them to take a challenge. They say something like, "We know that you are people of prayer. That you are committed to a life of prayer. We want to offer a challenge to you. Would you pray for one week in the name of Jesus Christ as you pray. Ask in His name for anything that is important to you, for just one week."

A few Muslims took them up on their challenge. The missionaries returned a week later to hear abundant news of prayers being answered, most for the first time. One man said, "I have been praying for years, and not one of my prayers has been answered. This week, praying in the name of Jesus Christ, each of my prayers was answered."

What if these people had not been willing to let go of their beliefs to try praying in a different name –to a more powerful name. To a God who is alive and cares about them. To a God who has the power to answer their prayers and delights to do so.

Pride keeps us from accepting another way: the "sprinkling of blood" way, the dipping in a different river way, the prayer to a different God. This all involves a letting go of pride and the beliefs that are "ways that lead to death" instead of life. The sprinkling of blood on the cross at Easter brought life and still brings life to this day.

My Personal Applications
for Embracing Easter:

When we were living in the High Sierras of California, I learned a very tangible lesson. Most of the neighbors living in our mountain neighborhood had at least one dog if not two or three. Our neighbor to the left, however, decided that they wanted to have some pet racoons. They invited a family of five racoons to live under their house. Each day they would hand-feed them an egg and also gave them dog food to eat. *(This really irked me because my family used to put on campfire programs for the campers in the summer who visited our resort town. One of the things we taught them was to NEVER feed wild animals. Our neighbors obviously never attended one of our campfire programs.)*

At first, this family of five racoons living in the neighborhood wasn't too bad except when the racoons would prowl at night they would attack the neighborhood cats. (How sad!) The number of racoons taking advantage of this ready-made source of food also increased to 15!

However, the problem really escalated (1000 times worse) when this neighbor decided to go on a three-month vacation in their motor home. They left their now 15 hand-fed domesticated racoons to fend for themselves.....and that they did.

Every night about 2:30 in the morning the racoons would wake up the entire neighborhood. You see, we had a Siberian Husky dog who had just given birth to puppies, and mama and puppies were living out on the front upstairs deck. I never knew if these hungry racoons would climb up the tree leading to the deck for the dog food or the puppies. After what they had done to the neighborhood cats, I could only imagine.

Whichever, mama dog wouldn't hear of either. Her howls woke up all of the other dogs in the neighborhood and soon the night was filled with howls and barks. No one could sleep through this, and soon we were so exhausted we met together to see what could be done. The next day, I went to the town's local animal control officer to ask for help. He gave me what's called a "Have a Heart" Trap. It is called that because it traps the animal, but it doesn't kill it.

I hope you can picture how this works as I describe it. It is a metal trap with bars so you can see inside. There is a platform where you put some bait to lure the racoon into the trap. Once he takes the bait, the door snaps shut, and he is trapped. He has taken the bait, and now he is captured in the trap.

Now why did I tell you this long story? It is very important to Easter as we talk about the "sprinkling of the blood." It all became clear to me when I discovered that the word for BAIT in scripture is the same word for OFFENSE. In other words, when we take the bait of an offense and don't forgive, we will be taken into the trap and the door will snap shut. We will be trapped in our unforgiveness.

What a powerful illustration! Jesus offered us a means to stay out of the trap. To be free. Because of Easter, He has offered us freedom through the sprinkling of His blood on the cross. He forgives us, and we now have the power to forgive others –to get out of the trap.

He challenges us to "forgive as freely as we have been forgiven." (Matthew 10:8)

Yet, as we know, many people won't accept it. They are left in the trap of unforgiveness and blindness to all that Jesus is offering to them. Many Christians are also caught in this trap. They look out longingly at other Christians wondering why they don't have the same freedom, love, joy, peace, and power as they do.

The answer is clear. They have taken the bait of offense and won't let go. They won't forgive or release another person from their offence. It has been bait to them.

In Matthew 6:15, scripture tells us if we don't forgive others, our heavenly Father won't forgive us. I never understood this verse until I experienced my racoon "bait and trap" ordeal. God loves me, but when we choose to stay offended by someone, with a lack of forgiveness, we are in a trap. Not free to receive all that God has to offer us.

The word for forgiveness also means release. When we release another person from their offense towards us, we are then free to receive everything that Easter means. I have had to forgive many people in my life over my 68 years, and each declaration of releasing them from their offense against me brought freedom to my soul. I learned all of this very tangibly because of some crazy neighbors who wanted pet racoons. God is so good and creative!

**Day 19
We Have The
Choice Like
Christ**

Forgiveness is a choice we all have to make, sometimes daily, and God has given us the freedom to make that choice. We can accept the "sprinkling of blood" on our lives for forgiveness, eternal life, and power to live in the here and now OR reject it and try to make it on our own.

Choices. God has given us the freedom to choose. He also gave Christ the freedom to choose. We have a choice to make and Christ had a choice to make.

Actually, choice was a part of the Easter story long before Christ came to earth. A huge part. Christ choose to leave the glory and the beauty of being in intimate presence with His Father to come down to earth. He knew He was coming to die, to pay for the sins of mankind as a sacrifice -- to offer a blood sacrifice, the sprinkling of blood.

That should tug at your heart. If you have ever read Prince and the Pauper by Mark Twain, you can see what life would be like if a person left his royal position to become of poor pauper. In this novel, they really don't make a choice to trade places, but through a set of bizarre situations it happens.

One of the boys, the former pauper, can't comprehend his new royal life and the other, the former prince, is aghast at the poverty, deceit, and evil he must face as a pauper. He had left the comfort of his palace and all of the glory of his position as the young prince.

Christ choose to leave the glory that was His life, his home. He knew that mankind needed Him. He knew He had an important task to complete for all of mankind and for His Father God.

In addition to dying at the end, He had the goal of spreading the Father's love all around while he was on earth for his short three-year ministry.

He chose. I believe His choice happened at creation or even before and not after the fall of man. God knew mankind would use their free will to go their own way. He knew the sacrifice would need to be made on mankind's behalf.

I can imagine the Father and Son in heaven during creation. Scripture tells us that they were together when God said, "Let US make man in our own image." (Gen. 1:26) In the course of creation with stars, moons, heavens, mountains, birds, reptiles, land animals, trees, and all that they created in the first five days, it was all declared good.

Then it came time to create mankind. I can just hear the Father saying to the Son, "Son, so far we have created a beautiful earth which is under our dominion. However, today the tide will change some. We are going to create a man, and later from him a woman. We will make them in our image and give them free choice. Sadly, they will use that choice to turn their backs on us.

Now we are creating them to have fellowship with us, but that fellowship will be seared because of their free choice to disobey. A holy and pure sacrifice will have to be sent to earth to rescue them. Son, I am asking you, are you willing to leave glory and die to save our creation. We can stop right here, Son. We don't have to create man, however, the joy of his fellowship would be sweet."

The son responded by declaring, "I will rescue them because I delight in them." (Ps. 18:19 - one of my life verses!) He didn't have to choose to experience this excruciating pain for us. His love caused him to say YES to the pain, the rejection, the mocking, the abandonment for a time from His father as He bore the sins of the world.......He said YES to the need. The onus is now on us to choose the "sprinkling."

My Personal Applications for Embracing Easter:

When I was a senior in high school, I said YES. I choose to invite Jesus to come into my life as my Savior and Lord. However, that was just the beginning of lots of smaller yet harder choices for me as I got older.

One of my mentors used to always tell me that "God is the blessed controller of all things." I John 4:6 tells us that God is love. John 3:16 tells us that we have a giving God who gave us His Son.

Yet there have been times in my life when the circumstances didn't match with the "loving blessed controller" picture of God to me. I had always been a "why asker" as a little girl. I guess I never outgrew that. That's why whenever something didn't seem "fair," I questioned God's love and His being a "blessed controller."

I felt, "What just happened to me wasn't blessed." It didn't seem like it would have been allowed to happen by someone who loved me. Losing my high school sweetheart to a drunk driver, losing one of my best friends to cancer, my husband losing his dream job, moving six times in seven years, my losing two jobs, rejection from a special friend.....oh, the list we can include so many times when love and life didn't seem to match up.

It is during these times, I had to choose. Do I live by faith that though these circumstances don't look like God is operating out of love or controlling as a blesser, He really is all of those things. The circumstances don't prove His love void or shallow.

I have a choice. Do I choose what I see or what I know? What I want to be or what actually is? Do I choose to live life by God's specs or by my own design. The choice is mine.

Someone once told me that as a child they loved the song, "Jesus loves me this I know, for the Bible tells me so." Then, they said.....life got hard. The choice to believe this sweet song was harder and harder to embrace.

I remember the day I was riding down the dirt roadway by our house to the neighbors 40 acres of raspberries. Since he has given us the freedom to pick to our hearts content, I was going down to check on the raspberries a few weeks before picking season would actually start.

As I was riding my bike (with no one around) I was singing out the chorus, "God is the blessed controller of all things! Yes, He is! Yes He is. God is the blessed controller of all things!!" (I Tim. 1:5)

Soon I arrived at the raspberry fields and was shocked to find that "my" beloved raspberries bushes had all been pulled out. The entire field was bare and plowed up.

Instantly I heard myself say, "So you aren't the blessed controller of all things. How could you take away my raspberries?" Then I realized what I had just said. How my heart had changed at the drop of a hat from praise to doubt.

How easily we turn on God when things don't go our way. We

make the choice to believe and then the choice to doubt. I immediately confessed my fickle attitude. (I admit, though, that it was a lot easier to take when I realized that he was just rotating 20 acres of the fields and not the entire 40 acres. We still have raspberries that summer from a lower field!

The freedom to choose is a delightful quality that the Lord has given us. It can get us into trouble or take us to new heights. I choose to live "sprinkled" by His blood even though I don't fully understand it or embrace that this is the way God designed faith to be lived. That is the foundational choice of all choices. No matter what, God is the loving and blessed controller of all things!

Day 20
Peter
Needed
Washing.

Just before Jesus was arrested, He had a precious time with His disciples in the upper room. They were sharing a meal when Jesus did something unheard of to His faithful followers.

He rose from the table, took off his outer clothes, picked up a towel and fastened it around His waist. Then He poured water into the basin and began to wash the disciples feet and to dry them with the towel that was around his waist.

When He came to Peter, Peter backed off saying, "Lord, are you going to wash my feet?" He was aghast that the Lord, His master, the Messiah, the One He had pledged His life to follow was going to do such a lowly job.

Jesus responded by saying to Peter that he didn't realize right at that moment what He was doing, but later he would understand. That answer didn't satisfy Peter. He told the Lord He would never let Him wash His feet. NEVER!

Jesus gently explained to Peter that unless he let Him wash him, he couldn't share in His fellowship. Sweet Peter then responded, "Then, please, not just my feet but my hands and my face as well." (John 13:1-17)

Peter realized his NEED. I feel there is the same confusion by many people about the "sprinkling of the blood" for the forgiveness of our sins. There is a movement today seen profusely on the college campuses to have no need for a savior. You see, if there is no right or wrong in the minds of young people, then there is no sin. If there is no sin, we don't need a savior.

Josh McDowell was a "soap box" preacher on college campuses back in the 70's and 80's. Since there is free speech on campuses (or used to be!), he was able to go onto a college campus and stand on a soap box in the middle of the campus and share the gospel of Jesus Christ. He would share how we are all sinners in need of a savior. In need of the "sprinkling of blood." In need of all that Easter offers.

Many responded and received the Lord. However, in this generation, since there are no absolutes, no definite right and wrong and each man defines his own pathway, there is no heart cry for a Savior. Admitting you have sin means to admit that there is a right and a wrong.

A movie of the Kennedy family's involvement in a car accident just hit the theaters at this writing. The one Kennedy brother says, "We will tell the truth, the truth as we see it." Right now in politics there are so many lies being told. Some say, "They lied. That is not the truth." No one seems phased. A lie is okay if the means justify the ends. Lying is not a sin when you can use it to obtain what you think is a worthy end.

It reminds me of the book of Judges where, "Everyone did what was right in his own eyes." (Judges 17:6 and 21:25)

The idea of needing a Savior who shed His blood for us on a cross is considered unimportant, at least on the surface. I know that many hearts are not seared. Many hearts still sense that they need a Savior to rescue them from themselves. In the meantime, "everyone is just doing whatever they feel is right with nothing considered wrong."

Only sinners need a Savior.
If nothing is sin, then there is no need
for a Savior. (How very sad!)

College kids want to be sprinkled with good times, free choice, wealth, popularity, admiration, easy grades, job offers, and the freedom to do as they please. "But that way leads to death." (Proverbs 14:12 and 16:25)

The cross and the "shedding of blood" has become a "stumbling block" (I Cor. 1:23) to their entering into faith in God. In their mind, the blood sacrifice stands in the way of their salvation because they don't feel they need saving.

However, there is power in the blood that they know nothing about- in the sprinkling of the blood shed on Calvary by a Savior who knows the condition of men's hearts. Who knows that without Him there is no peace. There cannot be real love or joy. The fruits of the Spirit are saved for those who believe.

My Personal Applications for Embracing Easter:

Now that I have been a Christian for fifty years, I can't really remember what it was like not having the Lord living in my heart. I can't recall what it was like not having a place to go for peace, a real source of joy, a genuine unconditional love, a fellowship with others who are not full of judgement or condemnation, being around people who choose kindness and goodness instead of selfish interests, and having inspiration from people who are full of faithfulness.

However, that is how I share the Lord with people in these times.

Scripture tells us that without the Lord we will know no peace. That there is a restlessness in the hearts of people who haven't allowed the power of the blood, the sprinkling of His blood, to come upon their lives. (Isaiah 48:22, 57:21, Jer. 6:14 and 8:11)

I have been known to say to someone who was sharing with me a horrendous situation they were facing, "I can understand how frustrating, even infuriating this situation is to you. I couldn't handle anything like that without my secret place."

That usually gets their attention. "What in the world are you talking about?"

I am talking about that place of peace in my heart that overpowers any circumstance. It's a peace that can't be explained, but it is a gift to me from my Heavenly Father God."

"Oh," they say. "So you are religious."

"Not really," I respond. "However, I do have a relationship with Jesus who knows what needing peace is all about and who can offer it to me in ways I can't even comprehend. I can go to Him anytime. He promised He will never leave me, and that He will give me a peace that surpasses any understanding, anything fathomable, within my heart. That's the only way I can get through this life that has thrown me some very fast and unexpected curve balls...like what you are going through right now." (Phil. 4:7)

How they respond depends upon the work of the Spirit in their lives and their openness to the gospel of Jesus Christ. Who doesn't want peace? It truly is the missing factor in every life that does not have Christ and the power of His Easter-shed blood in their lives.

Day 21
Surrendered
for Sprinkling

It is hard to comprehend how the Lord God could send His only begotten Son into the world in such a humble unconventional way. Born in a cave, laid in a feeding trough, visited not by royalty but by shepherds, having to flee for his life. We might say, "That's not the way I would have done it."

However, God had His reasons. Some we can speculate about, and others we will need to wait until Heaven to comprehend. In the same way, we really can't understand how God chose to use "blood" as the center of His rescue for mankind.

Those in the Old Testament might have questioned the whys and the means. It probably took quite a bit of surrendered faith on Moses' part to accept all of the sacrificial methods set up by God for the forgiveness of sin. The system was, in fact, quite involved.

The one thing we notice about "blood" as a sacrifice, God never intended these to involve human blood. When Cain slew Able, Cain had to pay deeply for his shedding of the blood of another human being. However, shedding the blood of animals was not only acceptable, it was the means and method for God's people to regain close standing with Him.

If you trace the history of God's people, you will see that blood has always been a part of God's relationship with His chosen people. When the Israelites were ready to flee from Egypt after God brought seven plagues on the land through Moses, He told His people to put the blood of a lamb across their door posts to mark that they were God's chosen.

If they obeyed in this, He would pass over them and not take the life of their first born child. If not, He could not promise protection for them. That "sprinkling of blood" was a sign of surrender, of faith, of trust, of obedience. God honored that.

Pharaoh, however, had no such blood protection. He did not sprinkle the blood over his doorpost and his first born son died along with a multitude of other first born sons in Egypt. This tragedy, to Egyptians, but not to Jews, finally changed Pharaoh's hardened heart to let the Israelites go from Egypt. The sprinkling of blood was a protector for God's people.

Blood sacrifices have always been the symbol of the surrender, gratitude, repentance, covenant and protection between us and our Father God. When I look at it emotionally, logically, practically, as a system for people to follow it just seems crude and unaesthetic. Yet it was the means to obey God and to receive all of His blessings. It is the center message of Easter.

My Personal Applications for Embracing Easter:

There have been many times in my life, before and after receiving the Lord Jesus Christ, where I have just had a raw look at what Christians believe. Many times I come up with more questions than answers. Why did God do this and not that?

I recently had the privilege of touring the life-sized replica of the ARK in Williamstown, Kentucky. It is amazing. As my nephew and I were walking through the realistic displays telling the story of life before and on the Ark, he asked, "I guess I don't understand why God didn't just tell Noah and his family to go up on a mountain top. Why the need for a world-wide flood."

Again, we can speculate. It is easy to explain God's love because I have experienced it in my life personally. Answered prayers, unexplained peace and joy, life transformations, character growth, needs met, and comfort provided, all prove to me beyond any doubt that there is a God. A God who created me, knows me, wants to allow Himself to be known by me, cares for me, knows the intimate thoughts and circumstances of my life, and who can do anything. He is God and I am not. What else can I say.

He is also a God who allows questions, but in those questions He wants to see us instilled with faith to trust His every decision. This does take a surrendered faith. A faith that doesn't need all of the answers – which is what makes it faith.

He has explained enough to me, shown me enough of his loving power in my life, taken care of our world, walked with mankind throughout history (and I love history!) to prove Himself worthy of my trust even in some issues that just seem irrational – such as the need for blood as a part of our worship of Him.

Over the years, I have learned to have what I call the "Flow of Faith." It took quite a bit of time and exposure to God to come to this place in my life. I was a fist raiser. If anything happened that I didn't like or feel was just or right, I raised my fist. This took place in my heart. I could feel myself saying, "I DON'T LIKE THIS!"

I have to admit, I tried to live the Christian life for years as a manipulator of God. I would tell Him what to do in my life. I would demand He "perform" for me...my way. I learned that God can work and speak to an open fist more than to a closed one.

There's been an amazing transformation in my life over my 50 years walking with the Lord. Now I have a "Flow of Faith." I say, "God must be up to something!" I release Him to do in my life and in the lives of others what He deems best instead of trying to manipulate, change, demand, control, and convince Him to see it my way. I see a total change in my heart when life hits me the "wrong way."

What is God up to in your life? You may not like it, but it will always lead to something good, just as the blood sacrifices lead to the ultimate shedding of blood of the Son of God for the sins of the world.

God doesn't do anything in isolation. Everything circles around a broader picture which we need to give Him the time to unfold. It may be months, weeks, days, centuries....or even an eternity. That position of having a "Flow of Faith" helps us travel through this time line of the Lord God, Creator of the Universe.

Day 22
Sprinkled on
the Altar!

In the Old Testament, the "sprinkled blood" was put upon an altar. There was always an altar involved when blood was sprinkled for the forgiveness of sin.

An altar is defined as a built structure where the surrender of something can take place. In the Old Testament, it was at first used to honor a meeting with the Most High God for instructions or as a place to show thanksgiving to God for His provision and protection.

There were so many acts of God's leaders "building an altar" after an event, it is almost as if God put building an altar to praise Him into our DNA. It was a physical means of giving our time and energy to worship the Lord.

We first see an altar being built when Noah and his family exited the ark. I am sure that after they saw God complete His promise to destroy the corrupt and violent world of that time and to spare their lives, thanksgiving and holy respect overcame them. What was their response? Build an altar!

You may not remember this, but God told Noah to bring two of every kind of animal aboard the Ark. However, He also told him to bring seven of the clean animals, not just one pair. When Noah built the thankfulness altar, as I call it, after he went safely through the flood, he took those extra clean animals and offered them on the altar to the Lord. (Six would be two pairs, a seventh was free to be sacrificed. God planned everything!)

This is the first blood sacrifice that we see in scripture. Then for many years, the altars were just used as honorary places to give thanks to God. No blood sacrifices were offered unless that part was not mentioned in scripture. However, these altars were used as a place to recommit their lives to the Lord.

For example, each time Abraham (then Abram) had a special encounter with God, he built an altar to the Lord. He used these altars as thanksgiving places and as a place to call upon the name of the Lord for help.

When God called upon Abraham to take his son Isaac and to offer him upon the altar, he obeyed. Offering a continual surrender of your life to the Lord was not foreign to those who walked with him during this time. I often wonder when he placed his son on the altar over the wood if he knew that God's plan of sacrifice was never to involve the shedding of the blood of a person (such as when Cain slew Able, and his brother's blood was upon him.).

It was not until Christ that a "man's" blood was shed. He was the only human sacrifice acceptable to God. Animals, yes, but a human sacrifice would never be holy, pure, or sinless. Only Jesus could fulfill the requirement of sinlessness.

All in all, in the overall picture of God's plan, this was a picture of the coming of Christ and His sacrifice for us. God provided an animal sacrifice for Abraham instead of having to sacrifice his son, just as God provided His Son for us.

You often wonder the thoughts and lessons that went through his son Isaac's mind when this event happened. Understandings that he took with him into manhood as he became a father. We see that he also built an altar to the Lord when God met with him and promised him that he would bless his descendants just as he had promised his father Abraham. Isaac had learned that you meet God in special ways at the altars that we build to Him.

Jacob, Isaac's son, also build an altar that he called "El-Elohe-Israel" meaning "The God of Israel" after he made it safely through to Canaan and after reconnecting with his possibly-hostile brother Esau. He stated that he wanted to honor God who "answered me in the day of my distress and has been with me wherever I have gone." (What a great motto for us to embrace.) When he moved on to Bethel, he also purposed to build an altar to the Lord in his new home.

Moses also built altars to the Lord. The first one he named "The Lord is my Banner." God had guided him out of Egypt and he was moving toward the promise land with God as His banner. It wasn't until the time he received the Ten Commandments that God instructed Moses in the necessity of the sacrifice of blood on the altar. (Exodus 20)

God wanted altars to be holy as they were signifying the place the Lord lived, so He gave Moses specific instructions. He was told to take half of the blood from the animals sacrificed and put it into basins. The other half was to be sprinkled on the altar. Other times the instructions included sprinkling the blood onto the people seeking forgiveness or onto the priests performing the ceremony.

Other times Moses was instructed to put some of the bull's blood on the horns of the altar and pour the rest at the base of the altar. When you see the many accounts of blood being sprinkled or even dumped at the altar, you realize how bloody a place these altars became in Moses' time. The shedding of blood was a common practice for the Israelites. Why the Jews later rejected the ultimate shedding of blood for the forgiveness of sins to the world is confusing to me.

God saw these sacrifices as soothing aromas presented before the Lord, not as something disgusting or to faint over like we might feel today. Each day – yes, every day – they were to offer up a bull as a sin offering for atonement. Each time, yes – each time – the priests had to purify the altar before the sacrifices were made. It took seven days to consecrate and purify the altar as an instrument

God could use for the cleansing from sin. God called the altar most holy and wanted His people to treat it as such. (Exodus 40:10)

God's instructions were very specific and quite involved. They ran from Exodus 24 to Exodus 40 including 17 chapters of instructions - where Moses did "just as the Lord had commanded." (40:32) How delighted he would have been to be present when the savior "paid it all once-for-all" on the cross. No more tedious rituals; no more blood sacrifices. Perhaps that is why God allowed Moses to visit Jesus at the transfiguration. What a joy that would have been for him.

Animals sacrifices had to be given day after day because animals cannot truly pay the penalty for sin. It was a temporary fix -- a sign of things to come that God used to point us to the significance and glory of the Lord's completing sacrifice on the cross. All of this pointing to Easter!

My Personal Applications
for Embracing Easter:

When the Israelites passed over the Jordan River under the leadership of Joshua, they were instructed to have one leader from each tribe to go back to the center and pick up a "stone of remembrance." "These stones will become a memorial to the sons of Israel forever." (Joshua 4:7)

Today, we don't have altars as they did in the Old Testament. We do go down the isle in a church to the altar to present our marriage vows. That is a time and a commitment we will never forget.

However, just because there are no holy altars for us to come to for repentance, we are given some ideas to create these times and places for ourselves. God never wants us to forget the ways in which He has acted on our behalf.

He tells David to recount the miracles God has done for him. It builds his faith and his courage. When he had to face Goliath, he remembered the way the Lord helped him win over the bear and the lion. Those were "altar miracles" – just the sort of thing we all need in our lives.

Jesus went away to be alone with the Lord God to pray. He didn't need an altar. He just needed an intentional time to be with God. I consider my desk in my office a place to meet with the Lord. The Lord is present there with me as I study His word. As I stand and look at this space and this desk, I get weepy thinking about the many times the Lord has taught me something new. He has met me at this "modern altar."

I created a prayer walk on the half-mile path near my home (yes, the one that leads to the raspberries), and as I walk it and talk to the Lord, I consider it a meeting place where the Lord is very present with me. Another "altar" place for me to be with God. It took intentionality for the people in Moses's time to plan and execute their animal sacrifices to the Lord, and just as they did this, we also need to be intentional about meeting with the Lord in "altar" places.

The men Joshua instructed the leaders from the twelve tribes to pick up the rocks from the center of the river after passing over the Jordan River, he placed them as an altar to dedicate the Israelites' new home. In similar fashion, we have done a dedication with each new home we have moved. We have dedicated it to the Lord as a place where He would live with us and welcome others into His presence there. I have small groups, speaker training classes, prayer groups, times with my husband, and family times – and for all of these the Lord is present. We made our home into an "altar."

Revelation 2:17 that tells us that God will "give a white stone to him who overcomes and a new name written on the stone which no one knows but he who received it." I love this verse, and I have a white stone that I keep at my kitchen sink window box. It is like an altar place that reminds me that I have given my life to the Lord and together we will overcome.

Coming before the altar for the "sprinkling of blood" has to be a choice -- an intentional choice. I love what my friend's grandson said to her when he prayed to receive Christ with her. "I am accepting Him because He accepted me."

I intentionally come before the "altars" in my life where God is present and waiting to meet with me each day. I am very thankful that my altars don't contain blood - that my Savior shed His blood and that part of the forgiveness plan from God is FINISHED.

That doesn't mean that "altars" are finished in our lives. Now we need the presence of the Lord where the "sprinkling of blood" is now symbolic and a remembrance of times past which set us free. Easter is a celebration of this time past that we take everyday into our future.

**Day 23
Coming into
the Presence
of the Lord**

Just as the temple and the tabernacle in the Old Testament were places the Lord came to be present with the people, the altar was a key part of this. In Leviticus 9:7, Aaron was told to COME NEAR to the altar to present a sin offering in order to make atonement for himself and for the people. Coming near to the presence of the Lord was also a common practice.

The Lord let his presence be known at the altar. In Lev. 9:24 it tells us that the Lord made fire come out to consume the burnt offering that had been placed on the altar. When the people saw this, they shouted and fell on their faces. They realized that the Lord had forgiven them. The Lord was present.

The sacrificial animal offered up had to be without spot or blemish. Not blind, maimed, fractured, with sores or scabs as it says in Leviticus 22:22.

After Moses died, Joshua built an altar to the Lord following the victories at Jericho and Ai. He followed all of the instructions Moses taught him. Each of the tribes followed suit as they conquered the various parts of the Promise Land.

In Joshua 22:28 there is a clarification of purposes for building altars. Some are for the priests to offer up animals for the forgiveness of sin. Other altars were build to be a witness of what the Lord has done, like the ones before Moses's time. It could be "a witness between us that the Lord is God, or as one that Gideon built saying "the Lord is Peace." (Judges 6:2)

Many altars were also built to false gods. In Judges 6, the men of the city tore down an altar built for Baal. Many Satanic groups have altars where they sacrifice animals as part of an evil ritual.

Saul also built an altar to the Lord. He had won several battles and before they went back into battle, he had the people bring animals sacrifices to present to the Lord. The Israelites accepted that the altar (blood and all) was a place where the Lord was very present.

David also built an altar to the Lord because there was a threat of a plague to come upon the people. David brought his offerings to the altar and as a result, "the Lord was moved by prayer for the land and the plague was held back from Israel." David knew that he would be heard as he approached the Lord at the altar. (II Samuel 24:25)

I Kings 3:4 tells us that Solomon offered a thousand burnt offerings on an altar before he started beginning his task of building the temple. The altar was a central feature in the temple which he had covered with gold.

It was by this altar that Solomon prayed his famous prayer in I Kings. When done with the prayer, he offered burnt, fat, and grain offerings for peace. Not only in his prayer but in his action of sacrifice, he proclaimed the presence of the Lord.

Most of us know the famous story in I Kings 18 where the people were crying out to Baal to answer them as they were leaping about the altar build for this false god. Elijah repaired the altar of the Lord which was near the altar of Baal, to make a point. The Lord is not with or present at the idols built for false gods. He is, however, very present and powerful at the altar built for the Lord God. To prove this point, Elijah has the men poured buckets and buckets of water on the altar and prayed to the Lord to start a fire on His altar.

You know the end of the story. A fire never started on the altar to Baal, but God's altar started with a mighty blaze. The false prophets were revealed and killed. God chooses where He will be present.

With a history of placing animal sacrifices and shedding the blood of animals as a temporary route to be forgiven from their sins, the Jews should have clung tightly to the final sacrifice of grace found in Jesus Christ, God's son. However, they rejected His being their Messiah and the savior for their sins. I find this hard to understand if they know anything of the history of their God.

Those who did receive Christ's gift of sacrifice, giving His life in payment for their sins, would have understood and grasped what Paul had to say in Romans 12:1. "Therefore, I urge you brethren by the mercies of God to present your bodies a living and holy sacrifce acceptable to God which is your spiritual service of worship."

Peter understood this as he declared, we were chosen "according to the foreknowledge of God the Father, by the sanctifying work of the Spirit, to obey Jesus Christ and be sprinkled with His blood. May grace and peace be yours in the fullest measure." And that it will if we approach the altars of our lives where God is very present.

My Personal Applications for Embracing Easter:

One of my favorite choruses contains these words: "Where the Spirit of the Lord is, there is peace. Where the Spirit of the Lord is, there is power. There is comfort in life's darkest hour, there is light and life, there is strength and power in the Spirit, in the Spirit of the Lord."

I often sing this when I need comfort. I treasure the Lord's presence in my life. What a thrill to think that the Almighty Lord God chooses to spend time with me. That He has gifted me with His Holy Spirit so that I can partner with Him in this broken world.

Whenever I speak at a retreat, I begin with a prayer inviting God into the building and into our hearts as we seek Him over the weekend. He always makes His presence known –- from the number of women who receive the Lord to those who make commitments to follow God more closely.

It also is seen in the women who chose to give up their false gods, their false idols and altars where God can't be present to come into the presence of the living altar of God! They have been going before idol altars, not the home of the true and living God. How glorious it is to see that they have changed addresses!!

The words REALIZATION and INTENTIONALITY stick out to me as I seek the presence of the Lord. I need a realization that my sin often keeps Him from being known to me. I build a wall between us that He wants to see broken down. He is always there, available to me. I am the one who moved. I am the one who built the wall between us. I just need to choose to repent, to realize my sin, and to allow the "sprinkling of His blood" to fall upon me.

This takes an intentional life style. One that listens for God to whisper (or even shout because at times I am stubborn) when I am going in the wrong direction. I love the illustration of the shepherd's staff. I had my husband build me a staff to use as a demonstration when I speak to groups. I share that there are two ends.

The staff has a crook at the top that is designed to rescue me when I get myself into trouble. I picture a lamb who wandered off falling into a crevasse in a rock formation and having the shepherd go after him like he did for the one of the ninety-nine. (Matthew 18:12) He reaches that staff down into the crevasse and lifts that wayward sheep up to safely.

That means so much to me because I always seem to get myself into trouble. Ps. 18:19 is my life verse: "He rescues me because He DELIGHTS IN ME!!" David who was rescued from so many poor choices proclaimed this verse. I have it written on my heart.

I believe this verse also refers to the Lord God rescuing us from sin on the cross as well as everyday needs. Peter knew that the Easter story is a rescue story when he said we would "obtain the outcome of our faith, the salvation of our souls" (I Peter I:9) because of our faith in the "sprinkling of the blood" into our lives from a willing Savior.

The straight part of the shepherd's staff is called the rod. It is used for correction. I picture the good shepherd gently tapping the sheep that is starting to go astray with the rod. It is a gentle caution that is often ignored. Then, when the sheep doesn't listen, the "tap" gets a little more emphatic.

As the sheep chooses to proceed to go his own way into danger, the taps get harder. Sometimes, the shepherd lets the sheep go his own way, but He is always ready to rescue him with the staff. The shepherd knows he will fall into a crevasse sooner or later.

Jesus died on the cross to provide for us the "sprinkling of blood" that would change our destinies and our daily walks for eternity. It takes the realization of sin and the intentionality of coming before His presence for rescue and forgiveness to fully embrace Easter as Peter knew it.

Day 24
A New
Conscience

Peter delighted in the New Covenant. His entire book of First Peter declares the glory and benefits of the New Covenant. No longer would we have to present blood sacrifices to the priests over and over again. Because of Jesus the ultimate once-for-all sacrifice was made and now our consciences would be renewed.

In the old Covenant there were regulations for divine worship and an earthly sanctuary/tabernacle, yet they could not accomplish all that God wanted to accomplish in and for us. In the New Covenant, through the "sprinkling" and shedding of blood on the cross by our Lord, God accomplished much more for us than any animal sacrifices could accomplish. These "much mores" are often not fully embraced and are beautifully expressed by Peter and the author of Hebrews.

I Peter 3:21 notes that baptism is not merely removing dirt from the flesh but is an appeal to God "for a good conscience" and this is accomplished through the death and resurrection of Jesus Christ. A conscience that is clear and good is now possible and is a goal of God for our lives because of Christ. It is part of what Christ won for us at the cross.

Referring to the old ways of animal sacrifices, Hebrews 9:9 states: "Both gifts and sacrifices were offered which cannot make the worshiper *perfect in conscience*." The word conscience there means "A soul able to distinguish between good and evil, prompting us to accept the good and shun the evil."

The word perfect does not refer to perfectionism, but to process toward completeness, to a finishing of something. In this case, our consciences. It means "to add what is yet wanting in order to render a thing full." Easter started this beautiful process in us.

The author of Hebrews asks for prayer that they would have a "good conscience" which would help them desire to conduct themselves honorably in all things. (13:18) We are in process to be complete in our consciences and this process began at Easter. "For by one offering (Christ), He has perfected for all time those who are being sanctified." (Hebrews 10:14)

It wasn't accomplished with the blood of animals as Hebrews 9:13 states. "For if the blood of goats and bulls and the ashes of a heifer sprinkling those who have been defiled sanctify for the cleansing of the flesh, how much more will the blood of Christ, who through the eternal Spirit offered Himself without blemish to God cleanse your conscience from dead works to serve the living God."

Because of Easter, we are now free from the dead life of works to win our salvation. It has been given to us as a gift full of grace with no condemnation.

Hebrews 9:28 claimed that "Christ was offered once to bear the sins of many and will appear a second time for salvation *without reference to sin* to those who eagerly await Him." Did you notice the words in italics? "Without reference to sin"

When He comes back, we don't have to prove that we have been to the altar for forgiveness or been sprinkled by the blood of animals. It is ours by the "sacrifice of Himself." (Hebrews 9:26) His shedding of blood covered all of our sins past, present and future.

The law gave us a "consciousness of sins" (Hebrews 10:2) but not the where-with-all to find freedom. The death of Christ gave us the freedom that we would not be condemned if we didn't always make the right choices.

Now it is easier to do what is right because.... "It was impossible for the blood of bulls and goats to take away sins." (Hebrews 10:4) The New Covenant "put God's laws upon our hearts and in our minds He wrote them."

Then He goes on to promise, "and their sins and their lawless deeds I will remember no more." (Hebrews 10:17 quoting Jeremiah 31:34) This is called the "new and living way." (Hebrews 10:20) This new conscience stimulates us to "love and good deeds." (Hebrews 10:24.

This all might seem a bit random, but it all fits together beautifully. What was, the sacrifice of animals, couldn't do all that God wanted for us. It was a temporary picture of what was to come. Christ's gift of Easter (death and resurrection) gave us more than just eternal life.

It gave us a challenge: "Let us draw near with a sincere heart in full assurance of faith having our hearts sprinkled clean from an evil conscience and our bodies washed with pure water." We are no longer sprinkled with blood, but now we are sprinkled clean in our hearts in our consciences." (Hebrews 10:22)

My Personal Applications for Embracing Easter:

I want to end this devotional with a victory cry giving praise to our Lord and Savior. I am so grateful to have the freedom from condemnation, but it took me a long time to own this....what Christ won for me at the cross.

Because of Easter, "there is now no condemnation for those who are in Christ Jesus." (Romans 8:1) If I sin and condemnation lands in my heart and mind accompanied by guilt and shame, then I have put Christ right back on the cross. Just like the priests who had to give sacrifices over and over again.

NO! The cross won GRACE for all of us who believe and receive the Lord's sacrifice on the cross. Satan would like nothing more than to put Christ right back on the cross. My responsibility is to own the freedom of grace that the cross won and CLAIM it instead of getting into a cycle of guilt and shame.

Let me share with you how this works. Let's say I have a sin that just haunts me. It defeats me time and time again. Some examples from my life would be my eating binges as well as judgementalism and pride.

How does this work? I go to the kitchen and eat not one but three bowls of ice cream. I'm a bit down, depressed, discouraged, and defeated! (A the D's Satan is delighted to have me feel.) If a person knows to do right and does not do it, to that person it is sin. (James 4:17) I know better, so this is sin for me. Satan is waiting and watching. He would love me to get into the grips of guilt and the downward cycle that brings.

However, I remember that Easter has won for me the freedom to fail, to not be perfect but in process. I need to own the sin, but not the condemnation. Satan wants me to think that I am bad and that food is bad. Anything to distract me from him and the schemes he pulls on me. I have learned that I am not bad. I am a sinner saved by such magnificent grace that my badness is knocked out of the ball park. Actually it is covered by the righteousness of Christ.

I don't have to fall into the downward spiral of guilt and disgrace. Disgrace means "being apart in a different direction than grace. Grace alone, however, means a total freedom from condem-nation). I vote to move toward grace. Claiming grace will move me away from guilt and into gratitude, and there is power in praise.

Instead of having an inward conversation to myself that goes like this: "You are so stupid. That was very bad of you. You always do this. You are so bad. There is no hope for you. How can I have loved food more than God. I'm just hopeless and bad." If I do this type of self-talk, then I am stuck. Satan has pulled me into his trap of negative thinking, guilt, and condemnation. Feeling this way, I probably won't be spurred to love and good works, but will want to go into isolation. Satan is loving this entire journey into the downward spiral moving to guilt instead of to grace.

However, now, because of Easter, I can say, "Oh dear Lord. I did it again. I chose food to comfort me instead of Your Spirit. Please forgive me. Right now, I whole heartedly grasp your grace. I grieve my choices. Thank you that you don't condemn me – that I am covered by your righteousness and not my own efforts to be righteous. I am so grateful for your death on the cross that finally once and for all paid for my sin. Thank you for Easter, Lord. Thank you for Easter."

When I do this, I picture Satan's angry face. He didn't get me. The cross got a hold of me instead. In my mind I picture Satan falling from heaven like Jesus said in Luke 10:18: "I was watching Satan fall from heaven like lighting." Easter defeated Satan so Satan doesn't have to defeat you. I hope my honesty here has been a blessing to you.

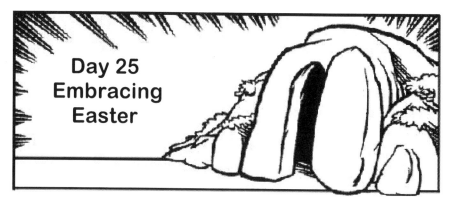

**Day 25
Embracing
Easter**

What a journey this has been to embrace Easter into our practical everyday lives as Peter embraced Easter. I hope you have been able to identify with the "scattered" areas of your life and how the "sprinkling of blood" of Easter can comfort our "suffering if necessary in diverse trials for a little while. (I Peter 1:6)

As mentioned before, God has a master plan. The Old Covenant with its temporary means of atoning for sin was part of that plan that lead us right into a beautiful understanding of the need for a Savior without spot of blemish, perfect in every way giving His life and shedding His blood for us on the cross.

This master plan is not yet finished. Like Peter said in I Peter 1:9, all of this is for the "salvation of your souls." It will all "result in praise and glory and honor at the revelation of Jesus Christ" when he comes again for us. (1:7)

In the mean time, He is asking us as He asked Peter to be over-comers. To bear up under persecution and trials. To let your faith be strong and even to be tested by fire. (1:7)

And in all of this God's grace and peace will be yours in fullest measure. (1:2) Peter got it. Even after his great defeats and failures, he was able to embrace the fullness of what Easter offered us. (Maybe that is why we have such great glimpses into Peter's struggling life. So we can never say, "I can't do this. My failure is too great."

There is no such thing as a 'failure too great" for a Savior who is greater than all of our sins. My failure has been great, but my Savior is greater than my sin and shame. I am in the process of embracing all that Easter won for me in the area of forgiveness and a pure conscience that seeks to do right.

That is all the Savior asks. God asks, "Will you?" to Jesus. Jesus said YES! God asks us, "Will you embrace all that my love has done for you?" I want to say YES! Yes to Christ! Yes to Easter! Yes to victory!

❧❧❧❧❧❧❧❧❧❧❧❧❧❧❧❧❧

I hope that you have been blessed by this Easter devotional. Please visit **www.FreshLookPublishing** for more of Christie's devotionals which include:

Secrets of the Soaring Eagle
Partnering With God
The Transformation of the Samaritan Woman
He Called Her Daughter
Elihu: The Faithful Friend of Job
25 Amazing Expressions of Christmas
The Delights of Christmas

Also for sale on Amazon are Christie's two new books:
When Godly Women Are Overweight: 7 Foundations for Change and 22 Myths We "Feed" Ourselves
and
50 Ways Out For Godly Women Who Are Overweight

You may contact her at
Christie@FreshLookThinking.com
❧❧❧❧❧❧❧❧❧❧❧❧❧❧❧❧❧

About the Author

Christie Miller is celebrating her 50th year of walking with the Lord.
Because of Easter, she has been able to....

Celebrate 40 years of marriage

and raisie two marvelous daughters

(by grace and God's marvelous intervention!),

Enjoy 37 years of teaching English

to kids in 4th-12th grades,

www.HomeSchoolLearningCoach.com

Delight in watching hundreds of kids over the years act in the 20 plus stage plays she has written and directed through her company Creative Youth Theater,

Www.CreativeYouthTheater.com

Minister as a Christian speaker to churches and retreat centers through her ministry Fresh Look Thinking and to train and encourage many Christian speakers while heading up Northwest Christian Speakers Bureau,
Www.NWSpeakers.com

And to realize the miraculous transformation that God has done in her life and continues to do because of Easter!

84938433R00060

Made in the USA
San Bernardino, CA
14 August 2018